What a **Billionaire** told a POOR Man

Patrick C. Anyatonwu

Copyright 2017
All rights reserved.
No part of this publication may be produced, stored in a retrieval system, or transmitted, in any form or by any means, electronic, mechanical, photocopying, recording, or otherwise, without the prior written permission of the publisher.

This book is not hundred percent fiction. But some of the names used therein are mental creations of the author. The authors quoted here are real. The places, incidents and monuments are fictitiously used, and except in case of historical fact. Any resemblance to actual persons, living or dead is purely coincidental.

Hence, the author or the publisher will not assume any responsibility whatsoever. Also the author or the publisher disclaims all liability in connection with the use of this book.

Printed by createspace.com

ISBN-13: 978-1548297497

ISBN-10: 1548297496

DEDICATION

To those who are willing to move out of their comfort zone.

CULLED FROM MAN AND MONEY

This slide is of an Indian origin. The author is unknown. It captures all I tried to do in this book. If you are not given to reading, just internalise the slide and you are good to go.

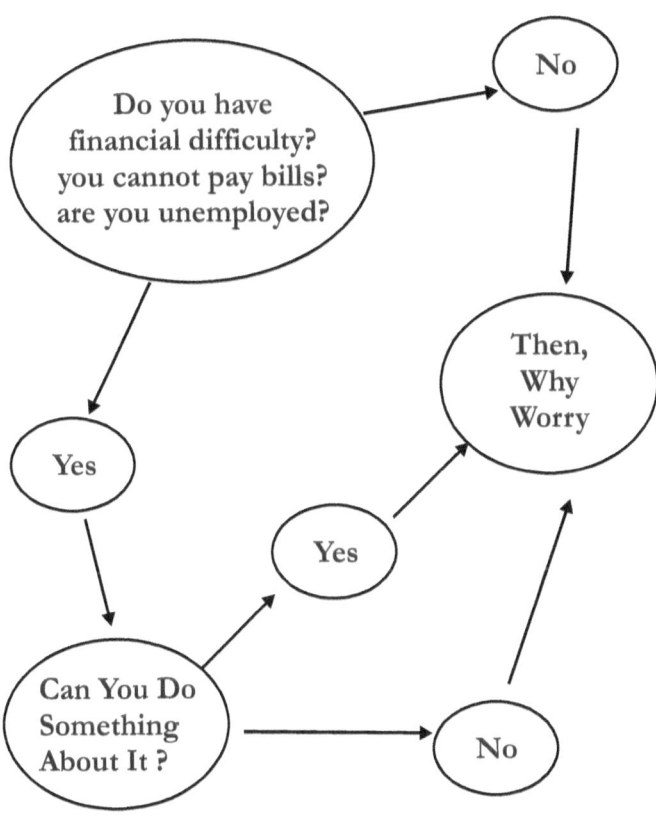

ACKNOWLEDGEMENT

> *"Any nation that decimates her middle class has entered into partnership with poverty"* - Patrick Anyatonwu, Author, Man and Money.

This book came to the physical equivalent because it was allowed by the Father.

To Him, I say thank you.

I must also acknowledge the support of my family. My wife, Ebele Pat-Anyatonwu allowed me considerable space without complaints. My only sister, Angela Ochie supported by prayers.

My kids, Master, Pharaoh, Oracle and Nwatakiri understood that Daddy was busy.

My typesetter, Ijeoma Ikeazota was always available to lend a helping hand.

Dr. Max Nduaguibe, Godfrey Okorie, Emeka Nkemdirim, put me under pressure to brace the tape.

Arc. Annes Audu and Achilleus Chud-Uchegbu followed me all through the period of writing this book. Every morning, the duo will call to find out if I had gone to press.

Ebere Nwaolikpe, Fred Nduka, Joseph Idegwu and Ifeanyi Uhuegbu were instrumental to the success of this project.

I doff my cap for kid proof readers, Pharaoh and

ACKNOWLEDGEMENT

Oracle Anyatonwu, who promised to introduce this book to their classmates.

My team at Forefathers Leasing delivered without supervision. I say thank you all.

PRAISE FOR PATRICK ANYATONWU AND WHAT A BILLIONAIRE TOLD A POOR MAN

This book, short and precise is written in a language as easily readable as anyone can write it.

Dr. Max Nduaguibe.

Success is not all about hard work; it is a mindset! The ability to succeed begins with creating the tomorrow of your dreams as a mental picture. This book, 'What a Billionaire told a Poor Man', exposes the mind to life principles that bring forth success. It is a must read for all success-oriented minds and even those who think they are already successful.

Lilian Njoku, Employer of Labour.

Patrick C. Anyatonwu uses a simple but captivating storyline; to illustrate that one sees fairer when standing on the shoulders of another who has gone higher. I recommend 'What a Billionaire Told a Poor Man' to every 'John' in a diligent search for a Billionaire!

Charles Chidiebere Ani, Social Commentator

This book from the stable of Patrick Anyatonwu ought to have come earlier. Written in a free flowing English, addresses the minds of many grappling with the onerous task of the next move that will provide them with bread and butter

Favour Abeke, Entrepreneur.

A must read for aspiring billionaires and entrepreneurs.

Ben Alaegbu, COO of BAE Turfs & Greens Nigeria - (Landscape Professionals)

My Boss, Patrick Anyatonwu has done it again. I was thinking that Man and Money was the best that will come from him but, I erred. This is terrific. Many will definitely benefit from reading this book.

Immaculata Udeozor, Financial Controller, Forefathers Leasing Limited

I have been a big fan of Patrick Anyatonwu's work for years. I was opportune to be one of the first to read 'What a Billionaire Told a Poor Man', and to be honest, Patrick has managed to deliver something better, something interactive and something different. Most financial books often come as a set of instructions, but, 'What a Billionaire Told a Poor Man' came in the form of a story and parables. I journeyed with this book and as I alighted, my financial skills and maturated. If you need a book on financial etiquette, I will strongly recommend that you read and keep a copy in your library.

Alimi Taiwo H. - A Digital Marketer.
CEO Alim Agency.

The gap between the rich and poor is becoming wider, with the middle class almost going into extinction. Hence, we need practical guidelines on how to close the ever widening gap. This book, 'What the Billionaire Told a Poor Man' is a perfect material for such a time. Patrick Anyatonwu presents simple, practical but concise steps on how to break out of the lower quadrant of life. I personally recommend this for everyone who wants a better financial future

Janet Mbakwe, Entrepreneur.

Patrick Anyatonwu is indeed a genius when it comes to matters relating to financial intelligence. In this concise and worthwhile book, he has explained in its simplest form, what qualities one should possess in order to attain success in life.

Ani Michael-Entertainment Expert (Mo'Ani).

What a masterpiece of a book whose author's humility is exemplified in the simplicity of the diction. No doubt, the articulated words of the Billionaire will jolt many 'Johns' of our society into economic freedom. Bravo, Patrick Anyatonwu. Another great work

Felix Ononeze, Lecturer
Alvan Ikeoku, College of Education

I wonder why Patrick Anyatonwu did not come up with this book early enough. I just wanted to glance at a few pages, but ended up going to work late. This book, 'What a Billionaire Told a Poor Man' is the missing key to move to the next level. I recommend this terrific book to young school leavers.

Nnenna Kalu, Customer Service Expert.

In this work, René Descartes' philosophical position, "cogito, ergo sum (Je pense, donc je suis/I think, therefore I am), finds resonance in Mahatma Ghandi's stance that man is but a product of his thoughts. What he thinks, he becomes. Hence, the capability and capacity of both success and failure lie in his hand. In this book, 'What a Billionaire Told a Poor Man, Patrick Anyatonwu robbed the principles of success even for the blind to feel.

Rev. Fr. Augustine Nwagbara.

This book charts the path towards a successful life and business. You would find it useful.

Lemmy Ughegbe, Journalist, Public Speaker & Mindset Trainer

TABLE OF CONTENTS

Dedication	3
Acknowledgement	7
Praise for Patrick C. Anyatonwu and What A Billionaire Told A Poor Man.	9
Foreword	17
Preface	19
How to read this book	23
What this book can do for you	25
Introduction	27
Synopsis	31

CHAPTER ONE   **49**

John learns the principle of persistence
Without which, there is no head way
Turned back several times
Disillusioned but persisted

CHAPTER TWO   **71**

John learns the principle of focus
Coming to terms with chief goal or purpose
Mind operations

Conscious mind
Subconscious mind
Affirmations/self-talk
The Power of words
Understanding self

CHAPTER THREE 83
John learns the principle of discipline
Asked to throw stone for sixty days
Reading and writing
Social media presence

CHAPTER FOUR 95
John learns the principle of integrity
The Billionaire tests John
Getting capital
You must learn to ask

CHAPTER FIVE 101
John learns the principle of savings
Habit formation
Delaying gratification
Financial intelligence
Investment
Money lending
Trading

CHAPTER SIX 107
John learns the principle of gratitude
The power of thank you
Asking

Team work and cooperation
Giving back

CHAPTER SEVEN — 113
John learns the principle of marketing
Being a Trader
Having a pleasing personality
Always learn peoples' names

CHAPTER EIGHT — 121
The Billionaire reveals self
How the Billionaire made his money
John goes to Harvard Business School
The Billionaire invites his lawyer
The Billionaire signs the Will

CHAPTER NINE — 125
The Billionaire and John part ways
Putting more than you take out
The body
The mind
The soul
Breathing
The duo sign agreement

References — 133

FOREWORD

In Christendom, the greatest feast is Easter celebration, yet 90 percent of Christians' that celebrate this great feast refuse to carry their crosses rather, seek only miracles to their problems. There is no Easter without the cross.

In my two scores of existence on this planet earth, I am surrounded by many people who blame their life and business failures on other people and superstitions. The good book says that the choices we make determine our destinations.

The majority of us can live a purposeful and wonderful life if we imbibe the principles inherent in the flow of nature, aptly captured in this fantastic piece of artistic work- 'What a Billionaire Told a Poor Man'.

The purpose of this book, hence, is to rekindle and expose you into nature and time tested principles of success in life and business, revealing the thin line between failure and success. The author, as always, has brought to bear on this book his rich and informed knowledge of hidden secrets, the order of nature and how to harness them for the good of all.

Patrick Anyatonwu, apart from being the former

Deputy Managing Director of Fortune Global and Logistics, a big player in the shipping industry worldwide, he is also Group Head at Forefathers Leasing Limited and a host of others that offer in practical terms these principles to small and medium scale businesses nationwide.

Patrick Anyatonwu is well known to me, and always calls me Boss at every opportunity, is a humble and well-focused family man.

I jumped at the offer to write this foreword to be part of a revolution that is about to happen in the knowledge industry. When his first major book 'Man and Money: the Hidden Secrets Revealed' surfaced, I erroneously concluded that Patrick has compressed all his wealth of experience acquired from many books by the world's best authors he read, still reading, and the businesses he has piloted over the years. But, I was very wrong. This second book 'What a Billionaire Told a Poor Man' is a dynamite of some sort. The principles are well delivered in a very simplistic, but powerful manner along with a captivating story format.

Patrick Anyatonwu is a natural teacher who tries to leave a lasting and a concrete impression on his listeners and readers.

I have read it, reread it and studied it. I have also profited therefrom. I highly recommend it to everyone who wants to succeed in business and life endeavours'.

Sir Cletus Obiajunwa Osueke (KSM)
Head of Practice
Obiajunwa Osueke & Co.

PREFACE

There are basic immutable laws for a successful life. Interestingly, these laws are the same independent of the faith we profess. But unfortunately, our world today is peopled majorly by an increasing number of mortals who erroneously think that these basic laws of success can be supplanted by religious rituals and perhaps even magic.

Everywhere around us, you hear people extolling the power of faith but without work and concerted plan. Yet, we have not seen people becoming medical doctors without medical training or lawyers without legal training.

The present day conception of the requirements for a successful life seems only to lie on persistent all day prayers, sometimes extending to vigils, lazy vocalization of mere wishes and thunderous vocal reception of priestly conferment from prayer contractors and all such men and women who prey on the gullible.

'What a Billionaire told a Poor Man' interrogates these anomalous assertions, in a clear and vivid, unique narrative style reinstating those very time tested and ancient principles of prayer and faith firmly laced with passion, discipline, patience, persistence, hard work, healthy habits and commitment that spurred our forebears to virtuous action.

The Author in his usual simple style, told the story in a very easy, quick to grasp method, exposing cleverly our own contemporary quick fix success tips which only end up in frustrating and truncating our efforts at making meaningful and enduring success of our lives.

Particularly, the expose on the role of the mind, conscious and subconscious is enthralling. For the young, this should be a useful manual to navigate the slippery terrain of the mine infested way to success. For the not too young and the elderly, this work is a veritable encourager, brewed to fire a new zeal and a fresh entrepreneurial impetus to go for it, knowing that it is never over until it is over.

Chief Chibuike Godwin Onyendilefu
(LL.B Hons, FHNR, CBD)
Senior, Special Assistant to the Governor of Abia State on Rural Orientation and Sensitization.

THOUGHTS OF PROFESSOR ABIOYE ISAAC

Recently, University of Port Harcourt sent off 5,473 students with 78 amongst them graduating with First Class.

Professor Abioye Isaac shocked the gathering with a speech that veered off from conventional talks. Many minds were immensely agitated, which eventually gave birth to a shift in mental paradigm.

What Professor did here within minutes captured all I laboured for over 1050 hours to do in this book.

Prof has made my job easier. If you can read and digest Prof's speech, then, you don't need to read further. But if you are the type that loves knowledge, read on and benefit from the Law of Compensation.

Professor Abioye Isaac, with your permission, I plant your speech here verbatim.

"Academic excellence is overrated! Did I just say that? Oh, yes, I said it.

Being top of your class does not necessarily guarantee that you will be at the top of life.

You could graduate as the best student in Finance but it doesn't mean you will make more money than everybody else.

The best graduating Law student does not necessarily become the best lawyer.

The fact is, life requires more than the ability to understand a concept memorize it and reproduce it in an exam.

School rewards people for their memory. Life rewards people for their imagination.

School rewards caution, life rewards daring.

School hails those who live by the rules. Life exalts those who break the rules and set new ones.

So do I mean people shouldn't study hard in school? Oh, no, you should. But don't sacrifice every other thing on the altar of First Class. Don't limit yourself to the classroom. Do something practical.

Take a leadership position

Start a business and fail. That's a better Entrepreneurship 101.

Join or start a club

Contest an election and lose. It will teach something Political Science 101 will not teach you.

Attend a seminar

Read books outside the scope of your course.

Go on missions and win a soul for eternal rewards....

Do something you believe in!

Think less of becoming an excellent student, but think more about becoming an excellent person. Make the world your classroom!"

"Keep your dreams alive. Understand to achieve anything requires faith and belief in yourself, vision, hard work, determination, and dedication. Remember all things are possible for those who believe"- Gail Devers

HOW TO READ THIS BOOK

> *"Through allowing, you become what you are; vast, spacious. You become whole. You are not a fragment anymore, which is how the ego perceives itself. Your true nature emerges, which is one with the nature of God"- Eckhart Tolle.*

What a Billionaire Told a Poor Man, is a small book on principles of running a business. But, it is delivered in a story format for easy reading. It covered almost all aspects of running any business.

It is designed for entrepreneurs and would-be entrepreneurs.

It contains nine chapters that are stitched together. From the synopsis to the last chapter is suspense soaked to engage the minds of the readers.

Behind the stories are powerful principles that its meaning might be lost if it is literally read as a story book.

After years of romancing literature, I have come to realize that people want to read what creates suspense and not knowing how it will end.

That I have done.

You have two options; either to rush the entire book and come back to study the principles or you read each chapter twice. It is designed to be a companion. Arising from the fact that we are living in a highly changing society where information hits our consciousness per second basis. The intention of the author would be defeated if this book is read without studying it.

Anybody that can barely read can benefit from this book. It does not require university education to read and profit therefrom.

Brethren, put these principles in use and watch the change that will happen in your life.

> *"Mind is the Master power that molds and makes,*
> *And Man is Mind, and evermore he takes,*
> *The tool of Thought, and, shaping what he wills,*
> *Brings forth a thousand joys, a thousand ills,*
> *He thinks in secret, and it comes to pass:*
> *Environment is but his looking glass"- James Allen.*

WHAT THIS BOOK CAN DO FOR YOU

- ✓ It teaches principle of success.
- ✓ It resets mindsets
- ✓ It brings to the fore how the mind works
- ✓ It teaches financial intelligence
- ✓ It teaches the importance of affirmation
- ✓ It teaches importance of reading and many more
- ✓ It teaches success principles
- ✓ It teaches healthy life styles

INTRODUCTION

> *"Keep your dreams alive. Understand to achieve anything requires faith and belief in yourself, vision, hard work, determination, and dedication. Remember all things are possible for those who believe"*
> *- Gail Devers*

Once upon a time is a powerful way of capturing the minds of children. Life has become so challenging that people are seeking for ways to relax their nerves.

It is a fait accompli that most powerful messages are relayed via stories, fables or parables.

Stories matter. Stories empower. Stories uplift. Stories humanize and convey messages more forcefully.

Generally, orators are respected by the way they carry audience along with powerful stories, allegories and parables. This is because storytelling has been scientifically-proven as a way to capture a listener's attention and hold it. Besides, it makes your message unforgettable.

All I did was just to latch into an already proven method to deliver a message that if put into practice would produce positive results.

'What a Billionaire Told a Poor Man' is a book that

What a Billionaire Told a Poor Man

the author figured out would capture the minds of many through a story line that is devoid of seriousness most books are known for. Man is fast losing interest in hard news.

John is a mental creation of the author and other characters therein. John was taught the principles and all-important dynamics of building business in a relaxed atmosphere.

Without knowing that you are reading a book that you would not have touched ordinarily, and before you know it, the book is consumed.

No matter whom you are, the moment you are serious to move to the next level, there are principles that you must inculcate and failure which, it might be too difficult to find your bearing.

From my experience not a few loathe 'hard news'.

They want it soft these days. This story book robs on the principles of the success without announcing it.

It is a book that anybody can read especially those who are newly setting out to conquer life entrepreneurially. It is a book to read, reread, studied, and practiced. In my almost five decade sojourn in planet earth, I have encountered many Johns'. They are disillusioned about life and oblivious of the next step to take.

Most of them veered off the tarmac and became burdens to the society at large.

It is hard to convince the Johns' of this world that there is life in reading books.

The importance of reading good books cannot be overemphasized. Readers are leaders. And, it is a sure

INTRODUCTION

way of avoiding the mistakes of our Forefathers.

This is however, made more difficult if after school, one is not only gainfully employed but not employed at all many years of graduation.

From available data, knowledge still remains what separates you from the next person. Do we need any one to tell us that the world has moved on to the knowledge economy?

You do to the extent that you know and two countries come to mind.

India and Cuba invested heavily in health care and today, countries all over the world are trouping to both countries for medical tourism.

The man of knowledge is valued in almost all climes.

Man is born with a blank mind or a clean slate and it is what you have picked from the five objective senses that will make or mar you.

'What a Billionaire Told a Poor Man' is a book that captured some principles of success which John passed through when his life almost came to a financial halt.

John was about to jump into a Lagoon before something strange happened on his way to the Golgotha.

Just like the Samarian woman who came to draw water from a 'Well' met Jesus, her life was changed for good. She ran out immediately to tell people about her encounter, so was John's. His encounter with a Billionaire was all he needed to cross to the other side of the divide. John, from the inside of him was desirous to change the course of his life after going

What a Billionaire Told a Poor Man

through most of the debilitating and life threatening episodes.

He desired it and he got it.

The Billionaire, however, took time to teach John some of the key principles of success.

Your life will never change until you change what you do daily. We are what we think all day long.

Sit back and consume what the billionaire told John.

SYNOPSIS

> *"Give me six hours to chop down a tree and I will spend the first four sharpening the axe"*
> *- Abraham Lincoln.*

John is a Nigerian. At 23 years of age, he graduated from one of the Nigerian universities. His father died when he was 10 years old. His mother saw him through school. During his National Youth Service Corps, his mother died mysteriously. Broken-hearted, he rushed home from Kastina to perform the burial rites. Money was alien to him as the Nigerian government was owing corpers three months' allowance arrears. Assisted by his friends and the maternal uncles, everything barely went well.

His mother was the third wife, and immediately after the burial, hostilities were unleashed against him. The environment was negatively charged. Being the only son, the other wives and half-brothers/sisters wanted him out of the way because of inheritance. His father was rich in real estate and nobody wanted him to partake in the sharing. Unfortunately, there was no Will to protect him. When hostilities reached a fever pitch, John had to leave the village to seek for greener pastures. He ran to his maternal uncle, who raised him some money to travel to any city of his choice.

What a Billionaire Told a Poor Man

Armed with some cash, he chose Lagos, which he has been told by some 'Eko' inhabitants as a land of possibilities.

On that faithful day, September 25, 2005, he set forth. Against paying for a full seat, he opted for an attachment and stood for over 11 hours that the journey lasted.

Hungry, tired and with swollen legs, John does not know any place to go to as the luxury bus announced the final bus stop at Jibowu-Yaba, Lagos. He slept in the park not knowing where the journey of life will take him to. Gazing to nowhere in particular and enveloped in deep thoughts, he murmured some prayers to his God and waited for mother luck to prove herself.

Hours passed and around 11am the next day, he strolled to buy some food, lo and behold, he saw his classmate Ambrose, he helped with some assignments during their undergraduate days.

Ambrose was happy to see his friend who was the best in the class. Many relied on John to solve complex mathematical assignments.

John is gifted, and solved algebraic equations just as hot knife handles butter. He was liked by both lecturers and students.

He was heading to a first class when his mother could not pay his school fees on time and he emerged with second class upper division.

Ambrose wanted a way to pay back, and after some exchange of pleasantries, Ambrose took his friend home. His parents were happy at least for the first time, Ambrose has brought somebody home as his

SYNOPSIS

friend. They welcomed him with open hands.

Everything went well. John was happy. There was food and a constant supply of electricity.

Three months after, Ambrose's cousin, Stephen visited, and that was not the first time he was visiting Ambrose in Lagos. Stephen was on the rough side of life and a cultist while at the university.

Ambrose parents never knew much about Stephen, but Ambrose knows that his cousin was not a gentleman, and he dares not tell them. Stephen was a chain smoker, gambler and a regular consumer of alcohol.

One day, as all left house for a church programme, Stephen pretended that he forgot something at home. He came back to the house, opened Ambrose father's room, ransacked everywhere and stole $1000 dollars from the wardrobe.

Quickly, he returned to the church and sat like a newly beatified saint. One week after, Ambrose's father declared the money missing. Everywhere was searched to no avail.

Ambrose's mother called him privately if he trusts his friend. He assured her that John was above board and cannot descend to the low level of stealing. Worst still, this was the first time money was missing in the house, and that was not the first time that Stephen has ever come visiting as well.

It was not a hard arithmetic to conclude that John might be the culprit. John was called in by the entire family after dinner. He was interrogated. He denied knowledge of the missing money. As the only

What a Billionaire Told a Poor Man

stranger in the house, he was accused of stealing the money.

The next day, he was asked to leave as the family would not harbour a 'thief'. With the worn out bag he came with, John left the house in tears. Where he was going, he did not know, but he had to go.

Ambrose cried profusely knowing fully well that his friend could not have stolen the money, but Stephen was likely to have committed the crime. And there was no evidence to nail Stephen.

Ambrose did not eat well in the preceding days as he grieved for the ejection of his good friend.

John became a wanderer

Devastated and debased, John became a wanderer. It was on a Friday that he left the house. He quickly made up his mind to attend any of the vigils that have become a ritual every Friday in Lagos. Luckily enough, Ambrose gave him some money to enable him feed for a couple of days. During the vigil, John prayed and cried. He pleaded with God to unmask whoever must have stolen the money of which he has been punished.

After the vigil, John went to one of the commercial garages at Oshodi, a suburb near Lagos. He narrated his ordeal to the chairman of the park who consoled him and asked him to brace up for the challenges ahead. Being a kind-hearted man, 'The Chair', as he is popularly called, gave John a temporary accommodation at the park and N300 for lunch.

SYNOPSIS

It was from there that John goes out to submit his curriculum vitae to companies. He attended multiple of interviews, and none was successful. Hunger was biting him harder. The chairman once in a while helped him with some money to enable him to buy bread and butter.

Ambrose visited

Before this time, Ambrose's father has sternly warned him never to have anything to do with his 'thief' friend. He threatened that any contact with John will lead to severe punishment and subsidy withdrawal. But, Ambrose was sure that his friend never stole any money and made up his mind to search for his friend. After one week of intensive search coupled with the fact that John's phone was not always functional. But, on one occasion, his line went through and Ambrose traced his friend to the garage with some clothes and money as he has got a job with one of the new generation banks. They cried and hugged each other. John was a shadow of himself as the school of life has done some devilish blows on his psyche. "Boyoyo", as he fondly calls Ambrose, did your father find out who stole that money I was accused of"? Ambrose pointed out that the moment he left; all investigations regarding the stolen money were dropped. John, however, assured his friend that in due course, the mastermind of that act would be disgraced. "But, I am happy that you never believed that I stole the money. I am

What a Billionaire Told a Poor Man

grateful to you", John added. Some hours later, Ambrose left, and it dawned on John that he was alone.

No mother, father and siblings. Many times, some negative thoughts have occupied the mind of John. He has one day contemplated suicide. He has always dismissed such thoughts and assured himself that climbing the ladder of success is around the corner. Besides, there was this burning desire in John that he would make it in life. Somewhere at the corner of his mind, John was sure that he would be wealthy but did not know how.

John became an 'Okada' rider

After many months of job searching, the chairman began to express some strains, it behooved on John to move on. He approached the chairman to buy him a tricycle on a hire purchase arrangement. The chairman declined and offered to buy a motorcycle instead.

John was meticulous and careful. Within five months, he completed the payment as agreed and change of ownership was perfected. Unknown to John, ill luck was knocked by the corner.

Again, misfortune knocked at John's door

Barely one month after John became the proud owner of motorcycle known as 'Okada' in local parlance; the Lagos State Government passed a resolution that motorcycle riding is banned in Lagos Metropolis. The

SYNOPSIS

policy stated that 'Okada' would be restricted only to the streets.

This, no doubt, was a heavy blow on the financial well-being of John. He had hitherto assured himself of riding the Okada for the next six months to enable him to clean up and find other means of livelihood befitting of a graduate that made a second class upper division.

As if bad luck was the middle name, someone hired his services to convey him to a bus terminal. On his way back, his Okada was confiscated by the Lagos State Government Task Force.

He rushed to the park and narrated his ordeal to the chairman who pulled some strings but to no avail. "Your Okada is gone", declared the chairman.

Once again, John dusted his CV

Okada has gone, he made up his mind to look for a more befitting job. He searched at every turn, he narrowly missed the mark. That night, John made up his mind to end the sufferings once and for all.

He assured himself that he has no mother, father nor siblings. Even if he dies, no one will look for him.

He planned to jump into the lagoon at the wee hours of the morning.

On his way to the Lagoon

Around 3am, John woke up and prepared to embark on his journey of no return. Quietly, he left his temporary abode without waking anybody up. He

What a Billionaire Told a Poor Man

convinced himself that his planned action was not offending anybody as it was his life he was about to take.

He was not interested in the concept of 'Heaven or Hell'. His mind was made. Commercial vehicles were yet to ply the road; hence, he trekked for the greater part of the journey.

Few minutes to the Lagoon, he met an old woman with a walking stick coming from the opposite direction. Fear gripped him. He felt that he has seen a ghost. Enveloped in fear, he wanted to run back. But, the old woman, in a trembling voice, said, "My son…., don't run away. Come! What is the matter? Have the gods brought you misfortune"?

Bewildered, John remained motionless as the old woman inched further.

Again, "my son", she said, "what have you come here to do at this unholy hour"? By this time John was almost transfigured, and cared less if was she was human or spirit. In his heart, since he has made up his mind to jump into the Lagoon, this woman might even make it faster. He expected the worst. The old woman sat by the pavement and beckoned him to do likewise.

The old woman brought out a torch light, flashed it on the face of John and smiled.

Gently, the old woman said, "my son, tell me the truth, what is your mission. Don't lie to me because I know the truth".

John initially was adamant, and hesitated to open up to the strange woman. He thundered, "old woman, who are you? What are you doing here as well? Were you

SYNOPSIS

sent to kill me"?

The old woman laughed and said, "My son, if I had wanted to kill you, I would have done that long time before you saw me. I have been watching you for long. When you left the commercial garage at 3am, I knew. I have been following you to this point". Perplexed, John thought for some time and told himself, perhaps, this old woman is a ghost or a spirit. Old woman, "John insisted, who you are? If you don't tell me who you are, I will get up and go as time is running against me".

Calmly and strongly, the old woman told John that he would not do any such thing as all matters would be resolved this morning. But, John realized that each time the old woman speaks, her words soothe his inner being.

"My son, I ask you, tell me everything, I might help". By this time, John was calm because physically, this old woman would not constitute any threat to him. He assured himself that if the old woman acts funny, he will just get up and accomplish his mission.

"My son, the mind of the youth is filled with possibilities. And, the moment these aspirations are not met immediately, the youth seems to be brash in his decisions and might even attempt to harm himself. Now, tell me, what is the matter"?

John opens up

John started from the beginning without omitting a single detail. The old woman listened with rapt attention without asking questions. After one hour of

What a Billionaire Told a Poor Man

narration, John started crying, about to be convulsed, but the old woman touched him in the forehead and encouraged him to finish his life story.
He gathered some courage, biting his lips to force back the tears.
When John finally finished his litany of woes, he was relieved. The old woman, who for the first time introduced herself as Mama Grace was silent for over five minutes which was like an eternity to John.
As the minutes crept by, John had no way of knowing if Mama Grace heard anything he said or if he has spent over hour talking to himself. Mama Grace heaved the sigh of relief and laughed, which to a large extent embarrassed John. "Does it mean that all I narrated is not enough to make this woman sympathize with me instead of laughing", he carried himself.
Mama Grace asked if that was all that was bothering him and he nodded. "But, what was your mission this early? Have you gotten a job or are the gods pursuing you"?
"Just tell me, what did you come out this early morning to do"? John told her that he wanted to jump into the Lagoon. She became silent. Gazed into the dark cloud and said nothing.
"Oh! She exclaimed. You planned to kill yourself? Who told you that where you are going you will find peace"? She continued. "My son, there is nothing you are passing through that those before you have not gone through. Had it been that anybody who, faced with life challenges killed himself/herself, you would not have met anybody here. This is your own

SYNOPSIS

opportunity to turn things around. You can do it if only you want to. You see, man is what he thinks of himself. If you think that you are a failure, you are. If you think that you are a success, you will be successful. The mental positive attitude is central to our well-being. Man is his greatest obstacle. He limits himself mentally. He builds road blocks in his brain and does everything to bring it to its physical equivalent. Haven't you heard about that scientist who tried to manufacture bulb and failed 1000 times? He did not give up. Today, we have electric bulb, and do you know the mental energy that was expended".

"You might think life is not fair to you, but anybody you see on the street has some challenges and nobody carries their problems on the foreheads. Young man, you must brace up and face yours because I am facing mine as well. Killing yourself is not an option, if you do that, who will others coming from behind learn from? You see, don't cut the chain of knowledge. You are here to do your part, and when your allotted time is up, you hand over the baton of life to others. And, assuming that there is life after death, there is the likelihood that your problems would follow you to the Lagoon. 'Nna' let's solve all we can here".

John was silent, he listened with keen interest for the first time since he met Mama Grace, he calmed down and his brain started working for the first time in weeks.

"Old woman, what will I do? I am going through heavy financial mess".

"No, don't call me old woman; call me Mama Grace, she admonished".

What a Billionaire Told a Poor Man

She offers to help him

"Young man, I am prepared to help you on one condition", and "what will that condition be", John retorted. "You must make up your mind that you must succeed. You must accept the fact from the inside of yourself that you were born to do well. You were born to do good and contribute your own quota to the society. You were fearfully and wonderfully made. Don't ever forget this. You must challenge yourself that you don't have any duplicate, and no force anywhere can stop you from succeeding once your mind is made up to do so. You are the original copy of John".

She continued. "Most people don't believe that there are secrets to attaining riches. They have immersed themselves with the mentality that only hard work pays. Yes, I agree that one needs to work hard but, you must enjoy what you do and have an undivided belief that success is near the corner. Anything outside this would be tantamount to running in circles".

"Have you heard about one of the authors of the old? His name was Napoleon Hill"?

"Yes, Mama Grace, I have".

"Good, he was reputed with a saying that a man can achieve whatever he makes up his mind to achieve only if he is convinced in his heart that he can. You will be an instant success the moment your mind, your thoughts and actions are in agreement".

She continued. "Once these are in place, you are on the road to success. At such height of conviction,

SYNOPSIS

negative thoughts will never occupy your mind. You will be geared towards what to do next because everything would have been spelt out.

"You see, my son, success is a journey. You must take the first step. Just like riding a bicycle, before you become proficient, you must have fallen a couple of times. These are laws of nature.

Nature is neutral. The laws would not be altered because, according to you, you are facing a lot of challenges. The only option you have is to cooperate with the laws of nature and move on. Have you ever observed a child who is learning how to walk for the first time in life"?

"Yes, Mama, I have".

"What did you notice", she demanded? John cleared his throat. "It was not easy for the child. He would get up several times and fell. Many times, he/she would sustain injury"

"Yes, my son, that is how life is structured. At every turn, there is a hurdle. It will be conquered by you and no other person. It is only when you make up your mind to succeed that a way will be provided for you. All you narrated you passed through was to prepare you for the challenges ahead. Successful people are successful because they never allowed temporary setbacks rob them of the crown.

When there is a will there will be a way. Once you make up your mind to succeed, find me and I will show you how".

John was hesitant. He gazed into the Lagoon and said nothing. Mama Grace picked her walking stick, and started her journey. "Young man, I have my own

What a Billionaire Told a Poor Man

issues to deal with and I have spent over one hour with you. I have other assignments. They must be attended to. May the gods of our ancestors protect and guide you as you continue to find your way to success. Bye".

John gazed into oblivion as Mama Grace walked away slowly but gently. He was there for seconds without knowing what else to do, while the old woman continued her journey slow and steady.

As if jolted by an inner prompting, John started calling Mama Grace, but she was far gone. Shouting at the tip of his voice, Mama Grace has gone out of hearing reach and he started pursuing her. After five minutes of hot chase, John came to a junction and without knowing which way the old woman followed, he started to sob. He blamed himself for his slowness in taking decision.

Years back, John had always suffered from the pangs of procrastination.

He prayed and shouted, but Mama Grace was nowhere to be found. He, however, dashed into the road on the left and ran as fast as he could, shout but, she was not in sight.

He rushed back to the junction to see if Mama Grace has appeared from her hiding place. According to his estimation, she could not have gone too far away.

Angry with himself, John once again, he ran South, North, East and West, still no sign of Mama Grace.

Unknown to John, she was sitting behind a shed as the day was still cloudy. She needed to see John's determination and conviction that he was ready to take up his life challenges as a man; she cleared her throat and feebly called out…… "My son, come over

SYNOPSIS

here". Startled with goose pimples all over his body, John looked left and right and enveloped by fear. He then sighted Mama Grace by the corner and ran to meet her.

He embraced her and cried profusely. Mama Grace consoled him. "Young man, I have been watching you run up and down. I wanted to make sure you have made up your mind and convinced that you're ready to move to the next level.

Now that your inner being is ready, I am going to help you find your bearing"

Now listen to me

"Young man, there is no likelihood that you will ever see me after today. My time is almost here. I will soon embark on a journey of which I am not sure I will return the same".

John became confused and admonished Mama Grace to stop talking in that manner. He begged her that fate has brought them together and would not want to lose her. "Remember that I am an orphan. I don't have anybody who speaks for me. I can't even enter my father's house. They don't want me around and might kill me, if I get closer.

Please Mama Grace, tarry with me while I navigate the vicissitudes of life. I need you to move on".

"Now, listen, I will introduce you to my younger brother. He is a rich man in all currencies of the world. His name is Chief Godfrey (the Billionaire). He lives in one of the most expensive areas of the Banana Island, Lagos. The crescent is owned by him.

What a Billionaire Told a Poor Man

Seeing him, might be difficult as he is surrounded by a coterie of combat-ready security details. You will see him, but it will take you some days, if not weeks to penetrate his fortress. I will pray for you. You will see him. You will be patient, perhaps, after a series of trials, he will see you. Narrate to him all you have passed through. Remember, never to hide information from him. He is kind hearted, but very impatient. He scarcely spends time on frivolities. But, my name is the only ticket that will open the door of his heart. We loved each other.

He will not be able to say no to me because I made him what he is today".

Mama Grace opened her worn-out bag, brought out N2000 and handed it over to John. "My son, take this money. Go home with it, buy some food, and prepare on how to meet with my younger brother.

Never allow anything at all to prevent you from going to my brother's house till he sees you.

Some challenges will come. Distractions will come. Your friends will discourage you. You will be frustrated. They will make a scorn of you at the gate".

"My son, persevere, there is always a light at the end of the tunnel. Negative influences and negative people will hold you down. On your road to success, you need to keep all the negativity outside of your walls. Make sure you surround yourself with the people you deem fit and who will help you get to where you want to. I have done my part; the rest is up to you. My time is almost here. I will continue to pray for you wherever I may be".

"One more thing, she continued. "If you think you

SYNOPSIS

can catch a fish without first learning the behaviour of fishes, you are simply a professional time waster"
They embraced each other once more and parted ways.
The next day, John sets out to see the Billionaire.

CHAPTER ONE

John Learns The Principle Of Persistence

> *"You may encounter many defeats, but you must not be defeated. In fact, it may be necessary to encounter the defeats, so you can know who you are, what you can rise from, how you can still come out of it"*
> *- Maya Angelou.*

John could not sleep well as he mentally planned how to meet with the Billionaire, and also was disturbed that Mama Grace said that "we loved each other". Does it mean that they don't love each other again? Whoever Mama Grace was, she was a good and kind woman with feelings.

He hadn't enough transport fare, so he set out by 4am when transport fares will be a little cheaper. And, because he had not been to that area of Lagos before, he reasoned that he might find it slightly difficult to locate the address given to him by Mama Grace coupled with the fact that it was also dark.

John was awed by the ambience that greeted his

What a Billionaire Told a Poor Man

sensibilities. The environment was serene with no sign of life only security personnel who intermittently opened, the pin hole to look outside.

John summoned courage to ask one of the security men who gladly pointed at the gate of the Billionaire. Just as Mama Grace pointed out, his brother is really wealthy judging from the architectural masterpiece that was strategically situated and lying in two acres of land.

He hesitated before knocking at the door. He checked his timepiece and it was 7.00 am on the dot and he decided to rap on the iron cast gate. He rapped a couple of times when Adamu in a baritone voice thundered, "whooooo is that this morning"?

John almost ran away. The tonality was not friendly at all. Blood rushed to his face region as some sweat gathered on his forehead.

Almost trembling, John weakly responded, "Sorry sir, my name is John and I want to see the Billionaire'. "Which Billionaire"? "I mean Chief Godfrey".

The security man became apprehensive because people rarely come to see the Billionaire with legs. He cocked his gun and asked the John to come in.

He summoned courage and entered the highly furnished security post. Other security men were strategically positioned. John scanned the ambience. He nodded his head with the inner conviction that the rich have the tendency of living longer than the Hoi polloi.

The Billionaire's architectural masterpiece was secluded among trees on one of the most exclusive streets, it had turrets, gables, dormers, balconies, a

John Learns The Principle Of Persistence

screened-in front porch, a freestanding garage, a gazebo, a pool, and formal gardens. A set of sagging wooden steps descended three threads from the door

Mentally assessing John, Adamu became more worried. John was looking extremely tensed and haggard. It was obvious even to the blind that John was looking internally troubled.

Despite the fact that it was still morning, John was sweating. Seeing how stressed he was, Adamu allowed him time to calm down. The security post was friendly occasioned by the 3.0 horsepower air conditioner doing its work.

After five minutes, Adamu started his interrogation. "Come young man, who did you say you are looking for"? John said that he has come to see the Billionaire. "But, do you know him in person"? "No". "Do you have any message for him"? "Yes". "Then, pass the message and go. The Billionaire takes time before he comes down stairs".

John said that he is prepared to wait no matter how long it takes the Billionaire to come down. Hearing this, Adamu asked, "who sent you and you are coming from where"?

John said that he came from Oshodi, a suburb near Lagos, and was sent by Mama Grace. Hearing Mama Grace Adamu jolted and exclaimed, "Mama Grace! Oh, do you know her? Where and when did you see her? What is your business with her? Where is she now? How are my sure that she sent you? Did she give you any note"? Too many questions at the same time and John did not know the particular question to answer first.

What a Billionaire Told a Poor Man

Mama Grace was the eldest sister of the Billionaire. She was one of the wealthiest women of her time. As a matter of fact, she trained the Billionaire and brought him to Lagos. What made Adamu more curious was that Mama Grace died two years ago and somebody is saying that the same woman that he attended her burial sent him.

But, because Mama Grace was a very kind woman, Adamu wanted to hear this strange story to the end coupled with the fact that Mama Grace facilitated the first son of Adamu to study in America. So, matters relating to Mama Grace must be taken seriously.

Besides, John never knew what was going through the mind of Adamu.

The biggest challenge being that Adamu did not know how to convey to the Billionaire that his late sister sent somebody to him.

As a security man, Adamu started another round of questions.

"Remind me your name again, please". He was treating John with measured courtesy. John was shocked that the harshness in his voice had vanished.

"My name is John", he answered. "Now tell me, who are you really and where did you meet Mama Grace"? For over 49 minutes, John narrated his ordeal to Adamu from his childhood to date. Adamu listened with undivided attention. "Ok, I have heard all your stories. Kindly describe Mama Grace to me".

John tried as much as he could describe her, leaving no details. Adamu was half convinced that John really met with the ghost of Mama Grace.

"John, tell me, was the woman you said you met

John Learns The Principle Of Persistence

hard, normal or slow spoken? This was the last test for Adamu to be fully convinced that he is not as well dealing with a ghost.

"Oga Adamu, Mama Grace is a slight stammerer. She draws her speech and never in a hurry to speak. In a simple language despite that she stutters at times, Mama is soft-spoken".

Then, Adamu told John that Mama Grace died two years ago and was buried one month after. "I was at the burial ceremony. Who is who in this country attended the event.

The Billionaire told the entire world that the fallen woman trained him, and made him who he is today. Nothing was spared in giving Mama a befitting burial. At this point John had almost lost consciousness. The hairs on his body stood up as shivers covered his entire body. He was just physically there. Adamu had to touch him to bring him back to life".

"Oga Adamu, you mean, that I met a ghost? You mean that the woman I met was long dead"? He started to sob. This is because, in his culture, nobody sees a spirit and remains alive. For him, his time was up as he must definitely die.

But Adamu assured him that Mama Grace was almost a saint and will never raise a finger to hurt him. She was in the mold of Mother Theresa of Calcutta in India, who shook the world with kindness. "Mama Grace lived for others. Her kindness touched every life that came in contact with her. Don't be afraid. Nothing will happen to you, if ever, not from Mama Grace. Adamu offered a glass of cool water to John to enable him calm down. He went on to tell John how

What a Billionaire Told a Poor Man

Mama Grace wanted to help one lady who served her conscientiously. That lady was very nice. She was Mama's eyes in the house and highly responsible. She was more than a personal assistant to Mama Grace. She was in charge of all Mama Grace's domestic affairs.

Mama Grace wanted to send her abroad for studies, before she fell in love with one man. I have forgotten the name of the man. To compound issues, this man was married with two other wives and was going to be the third wife. John's brain became highly receptive, looking for clues to match his narrative. "But, you cannot remember the name of this lady you are talking about"? "Don't worry. I will give you her name a little while.

Mama Grace did everything possible to discourage this lady from marrying into a polygamous home. All fell on deaf ears".

Adamu continued. "Many believed that the lady was under a spell, because, it was strange for a beautiful lady whose prospects were high and about to proceed to the United States of America for studies to abandon it for a marriage that does not match. Mama Grace could not do much because she has already given her consent for the marriage. It was then that, Mama Grace turned her back on her. Yes, yes…, her name was Agnes. Yes, I am sure". On mentioning Agnes, John started crying hysterically, and refused to be consoled. After a while he calmed down and became distant from the immediate environment.

"Oga Adamu, what else do you know about Agnes"? "You see, it is a long time now. I think the

John Learns The Principle Of Persistence

husband mysteriously died. Agnes had a son and later died".

On hearing all these, John fainted. Adamu was confused. "What must have led to the fainting of the boy"? Adamu removed John's clothes and sprinkled cold water on him and allowed him time to bounce back to life.

Thirty minutes later, John came back to life. "Young man, what is wrong with you? 'Kai' get up and go before you cause a problem for me. You came here with a strange story and now you want to die on my hands. You must go now. If you don't go now, I will move you. Get up and do it fast".

Seeing the seriousness in Adamu's eyes, John sprang to his feet and made for the gate.

Adamu escorted him out of the gate and bolted the entrance. John became confused and at a loss for the next line of action. He sat at the corner of the gate, and gazed at no place in particular. His mind has digested so much information in a few hours. "First, the woman I met on my way to Lagos Lagoon was a ghost but a benevolent one.

Second, the lady that served this ghost was my mother.

Third, I am the son of that woman. Everything was happening at the same time. Mentally, he prayed to his God.

John assured himself that just few days ago; he was headed to the Lagoon to end it all. "I was almost dead. Mama Grace saved me and brought me here. My mother served Mama Grace well. At least from what Adamu has said, my mother was a good woman of

What a Billionaire Told a Poor Man

which I can attest to it.

Throughout the life of my mother, she never quarreled with anybody either man or woman. I have nothing to lose to go back to that gate and tell Adamu that I am the son of Agnes. His mind made, he sprang to his feet with a strange vigour, and he knocked with confidence at the gate. As usual, Adamu answered, "Who is that. "I am John. Kindly open the gate and I will tell you something". Adamu was even surprised at the level of confidence that John was talking to him. He scanned around if John has brought some bad boys to attack him. He surveyed and he was still alone.

"John, have you not gone? 'Shebi', I asked you to go thy way? What is it this time? Have you come with another story? For the last time, I warn you. Any other knock on that gate, you are a dead man".

John dismissed the threat. In his mind, it does not matter if death comes from the barrel of a gun or from a Lagoon. Death is death. He mentally told himself that this is his last opportunity to be alive or perish. After all, I saw a ghost and I did not die. Who then is Adamu that I should be afraid of? The confidence has already reached an all-time high. As he hesitated, the subconscious mind urged him on as he remembered the words of Mama Grace. He picked a stone on the floor and with that boldness; he knocked with assurance that Adamu must open the gate. "Adamu answered, who is that please"?

John was surprised that he put 'please' in his response. "Oga Adamu, I just want to tell you something and I will be gone. Just help me". Swinging the pedestrian gate open John walked in. Adamu

John Learns The Principle Of Persistence

covered him with the gun assuring himself that any false move from him, he is dead. "Yes, what is it"? Adamu demanded? "I am the only son of Agnes. It was me she gave birth to. I know the story of my mother, I can tell you everything as my mother told me". If it was not the fact that Adamu was a skilled marksman, his Ak47 rifle would have fallen off his hand. Beckoning John to sit down, Adamu patiently listened as he narrated all the stories about Agnes. Once again, he was convinced that John was the only son of Agnes. "But, why didn't you say so from beginning that you are her son", he queried.

"In that situation, you will see the Billionaire. But, let me warn you, the Billionaire is a busy man. He is impatient with those that do not know what they want from life. He does not give a second chance. Here and office are like a Mecca. His life is so organized that each minute is allocated. Meetings abound both here and abroad. You are even lucky; The Billionaire just came back last night from a business trip in Europe. He went to five countries. Do not worry, I will assist you to see the Billionaire", Adamu assured John. It was around 1pm when the Billionaire came out of the balcony to scan the environment and to make sure that most things are in place and everybody at his duty post. Unknown to John, the Billionaire has watched all the drama between him and Adamu for over two hours and marveled at his level of confidence.

On sighting the Billionaire, Adamu rushed and gave him compliments. And five minutes after, the

What a Billionaire Told a Poor Man

Billionaire called Adamu to ascertain if there are people waiting for him, he briefed him about John. The Billionaire listened and said nothing.

"Did he actually say that he saw my sister Grace? This must be a strange boy. Anyway, ask him to wait, I will see him".

Meanwhile, have you offered him anything? "No, sir, it has been just water". "Now get the kitchen department to prepare his lunch. Endeavour to ask him what he wants to eat". "Ok Sir," he saluted the Billionaire and dashed out. Adamu came back to the security post and John smiled. He has made up his mind that he must see the Billionaire no matter what it takes. The build ups are too strange to be left unfulfilled. "For me, my mind is made. The Billionaire, the younger brother of Mama Grace must see me, this is a goal that must be accomplished otherwise I perish. Mama Grace sent me here and I must make her happy wherever she may be even as Adamu told me that she died two years ago. That is his business. I am on a mission. Nothing stands in my way. Mama Grace warned me. She said that I should never allow distraction of any kind to dissuade me from meeting the Billionaire no matter how difficult. I cannot afford to disappoint her, and not after she saved me from jumping into the Lagoon. There must be a purpose. In any case, I am here to see the Billionaire period". Adamu smiled back at John. "It is like the Billionaire is happy today. You are lucky. He said that he will see you. John, you must be hungry by now, what are you going to eat"? John did not waste

John Learns The Principle Of Persistence

time in responding. 'Eba' please what soup do you want and what kind of protein would you want'?

John was not interested in all of these; all he wanted was to fill up his empty stomach.

He told Adamu that any soup and protein will do. Adamu did not want to bother him again. He called the kitchen to prepare 'egusi' soup, 'eba' with fresh fish for one person. The line clicked and went dead. By this time, John was calm. All the fears have disappeared from him. He was exuding confidence. He was literally baptized with new strength. Thirty five minutes later, John was ushered into a visitor's dining table. He was perplexed at the aura around the dinning arena. Everything was in place. The wallpapers, the painting, artifacts and smooth screened walls. This is the first time John has ever been exposed to this kind of environment. He convinced himself that he must be legally rich as the orderliness and promptness of service have taken root in his subconscious. He was internally happy. He said his prayers and consumed the delicacy. Perhaps, one of his best meals he has eaten in recent times. Though, his mother was a wonderful cook, but the environment was different. He assured himself, his mother would have cooked better with the kind of ingredients poured therein. He made his way back to the security post to join Adamu. This time, they were talking as friends. The Billionaire observed John all through he ate unknown to him.

All these while, John has never sighted the Billionaire, but has seen his pictures everywhere in the house. Around 4.30pm, the Billionaire drove out, but

What a Billionaire Told a Poor Man

however, passed a message to John that he will see him when he comes back. This was not to be. Shortly after 6pm, the phone at the security post rang. Adamu picked and almost saluted the phone box. All John heard was, yes sir! Yes, sir! Yes, sir! Afterwards, he informed John that the Billionaire will not be coming back early. He was asked to come back the next day by 9am prompt. John almost trekked back to the garage until he saw a kind hearted man that gave him a lift.

Exhausted but not hungry, he went and asked the chairman if any of his friends will be going to Banana Island the following day. The chairman promised to help. Moments later, he told John that his friend would be going to that area by 5 am prompt. John mentally checked what he will be doing from 6am to 9 am when he was asked to meet with the Billionaire. Since he had limited options, he agreed to join the chairman's friend by 5am. By that time in Lagos, traffic is always light and less than one hour he was on Banana Island. But his challenge was what he will be doing to burn time as it was too early to knock at the Billionaire's gate as appointment time was 9 am. Luckily for him, there was a car mat around the vicinity. He approached the security personnel, who allowed him to wait in their premises. Exactly, 8.50 am, John was in front of the Billionaire's gate. Without much ado, Adamu happily flung open the gate and ushered him in. The Billionaire was keen to know the exact time John will arrive. He was happy that few minutes of the agreed time, John made it. To the Billionaire, he has passed the first hurdle of

John Learns The Principle Of Persistence

punctuality which, according to those that know him privately, he has zero tolerance to late coming. Viewing the security post via CCTV camera, the Billionaire smiled. "My sister must have seen some hidden qualities in this young lad for her to have sent him to me. As an ardent Catholic, I don't have any doubt that there is life after death. It is possible that my sister met with this boy. Time will tell". The Billionaire called Adamu to send word to the kitchen to prepare breakfast for two. The Billionaire's Personal Assistant was handy to handle all logistics. Thirty minutes after, breakfast served by the cook- toasted bread, wheat bread, plantain, fried egg, two packs of juice, two glasses of fresh juice, coffee, Lipton and two plates of fruits. The cook placed all in different bowls and designer's plates. The Billionaire's tea cup was gold plated. Then, the Billionaire beckoned on his PA to physically fetch John.

John meets the Billionaire

Moments later, John was ushered into the best architectural masterpieces he had ever set his eyes even on television. John came face to face with the trappings of wealth. As John sat facing the Billionaire, a single light burned, casting light on a chintz couch and an antique Quaker chair Improvised kitchenette off to one side Walls and ceilings were covered with mirrors, a high-tech bordello. Furnishings were expensive, black-painted. An old tape deck and a towering set of speakers whose cloth was fraying

He could not hide his bewilderment. His emotions

What a Billionaire Told a Poor Man

betrayed him. He imagined if it was this kind of the place that his mother lived before she eloped with his father.

The Billionaire allowed him time to savour all the painting and designs.

The Billionaire cleared his throat. "Young man, what is your name"? Without hesitation, John genuflected and respectfully answered.

"My name is John Benson Sir". "Alright, this is breakfast time. We will talk after breakfast". This is because, the Billionaire has the habit of having an eye contact, each time he is having a discussion with someone for the first time.

The breakfast lasted for 40 minutes and the Billionaire never said much.

The Billionaire is a slow eater. He chews every morsel that entered his mouth. The duo sat for five minutes in silence. The Billionaire casually asked John if he has learnt how to drink water 30 minutes before and 30 minutes after food.

"You see, young man, personal victory precedes public victory. Everybody must be able to challenge himself and herself.

Anyway, I have heard so many stories about you from my private staff. I need time to rest. Let us meet again by 1pm in my library". John was about to ask where the library was, but the Billionaire reading his mind said, "My personal assistant will fetch you shortly before time.

For now, you can go to the reception. There is couple of magazines and newspapers you can occupy your mind with or you can join Adamu at the security

John Learns The Principle Of Persistence

post.

The Billionaire wanted to test John if he prefers idling away with feeding his mind.

For the second time, John passed. He chose to stay in the reception.

The Billionaire learnt very early in life that reading is one of the ways that the poor can climb the ladder of success, all things being equal.

As John made for the door, the Billionaire called him back. "I have this little book titled 'Think and Grow Rich' by Napoleon Hill at the right flank of the shelf. If you don't mind, flip through it until we meet by 1pm".

Again, the Billionaire gave John another hurdle to pass.

Few minutes to 1pm, John emerged from the reception, armed with the book the Billionaire recommended.

On sighting John, the PA immediately escorted him to a massive library where the Billionaire was already seated.

"Hello young man, it is like you have mastered the art of keeping to time. This is a good virtue that is capable of opening doors for you.

Kindly remind me your name again", the Billionaire continued. "Sir, my name is John Benson". Ok, I will not forget again. I love peoples' names. Alright, what is it that you want to tell me about? But unfortunately, I am rushing to a meeting now. We won't be able to talk now , but some other time. Besides, were you able to open the book I told you to flip through"? "Yes sir", John, answered; "I am

What a Billionaire Told a Poor Man

already in chapter two".

"Good", the Billionaire nodded. John was absent minded as he gazed at the stacked books, mainly on marketing, finance, accounting, economics, inspirational, tourism, hotel management, motivational, leadership, mentorship, encyclopedia, biographies, autobiographies and couple of other books. There were many versions Holy Bible and Quran.

John was almost lost in thought when the Billionaire gently woke him up from his momentary trance.

The Billionaire probed, "it is like you like books"? "Yes, sir, I am in love with books". "It is okay, I will leave you here".

He pressed the table bell and within seconds the PA appeared as if he knew he would be called. "Allow John to stay here for sometimes and instruct the cook to prepare lunch for him as I am almost on my way out. Ask my driver to pull out the white Rolls Royce". He gave compliments and disappeared.

The Billionaire enjoined John to make himself comfortable, promising to be back at 6pm.

John buried himself in the books and lost conscious of time. It was not until 4:30pm that he realized that lunch has been prepared for him. He came out and rushed to the visitor's dining room. The food was already getting cold. Within minutes, he rushed back to the library. Meanwhile, the Billionaire left his CCTV camera on. It recorded all the activities of John while he was away.

By exactly 6pm, the Billionaires drove in.

John Learns The Principle Of Persistence

Immediately he alighted from the vehicle, he asked of John. He was told that he is in the library, he once again nodded head.

He went to his room and replayed the CCTV camera. He became convinced that John can be trained no matter what he was currently facing. Nobody was born a champion. My sister was instrumental to what I am today.

I will do my best to encourage John since he has shown signs of seriousness. First, he has learnt how to keep to time and loves to read. The combination of the two qualities is an ingredient one needs to survive.

"Young man, The Billionaire said, how was your day? Were you able to find new principles you can put in real life from what you have studied today"? John nodded in affirmation.

"John", he addressed him by his first name for the first time. "You see, I am tired now; we will not be able to talk. I know that you have enough to say about, but I am extremely exhausted to listen to you.

The Billionaire studied John with the corner of his eyes to see if John will betray any sign of irritation. But, not John, he kept his face expressionless, not after going through all the pains in his short life.

For him, he reasoned, any other place would be better than the Lagoon. In contrast, the Billionaire's house is a 'heaven' on earth, even though I don't know how long my stay will be, he thought. The Billionaire asked John if he could pass a night to enable them have a lengthy discussion in the morning of which he gladly accepted with open hands.

The Billionaire pressed the bell and the PA

What a Billionaire Told a Poor Man

surfaced like lightening. He gave the Billionaire compliments and waited for instructions. "Get the porters to prepare Room 5 as my guest will not be going today, the assistant rushed out to carry out the instructions.

John, though, why would the Billionaire choose Room 5? He has heard stories how "Big men" kill poor people for sacrifices. But he assured himself that if he did not meet Mama Grace on his way to the Lagoon, he would have been long gone by now. Perhaps, the Sharks would have made a meal of me.

However, the Billionaire chose room 5 because his window is directly opposite. He wanted to find out when John would switch off the lights.

Being an avid reader himself, he hates people who do not read.

Forty one minutes after, the Billionaire and John were seated at the dinner table. The cook never asked the Billionaire what he will be having for dinner as he always knows that he eats light meals every night. He brought Quaker oats, four slices of wheat bread, plenty of vegetables and fruits. He also brought pounded yam and Semolina apparently suspecting that John will choose heavy meal.

The Billionaire did not say much. After the meal, he engaged John in current affairs, politics, political economy and governance generally.

Afterwards, the duo parted ways. The PA took John to his temporary abode. He was impressed with the furnishing. Everything was in place. The pillow was made of feather. The foam was body-friendly. John mentally thanked Mama Grace for saving his life.

John Learns The Principle Of Persistence

The Billionaire intermittently looked through the window to see if he was still awake and he was. He nodded his head, and assumed that he must have been reading because he saw he took a couple of books from the library.

In the morning, the Billionaire sent for John, and once again, he postponed their meeting till next day. He casually told John that he forgot that he would be having a board meeting with his foreign partners by 11am.

He offered John to go and come back the next day if he so wishes or stays back and use the library. John opted to stay back. The Billionaire nodded, but kept his face expressionless.

All these while, the Billionaire was testing John on the principle of persistence. The Billionaire learnt early in life that the principle of persistence and perseverance are twin principles that will catapult a slave to a landowner.

The Billionaire and John finally had discussed

The Billionaire was home by 4pm and immediately sent for John, who was still in the library. The duo went straight to the Billionaire's thinking room. The room is sparsely furnished but acoustically treated

Noise does not permeate. No electric bulb, but lamp. The Billionaire goes to the thinking room to solve some challenging business issues.

"John, I am here now for the discussion. I have tested you if you will show signs of impatience and irritation which is synonymous with the youth. But

What a Billionaire Told a Poor Man

you have shown that you are positively wired.

He told him everything without holding back a single detail. The Billionaire listened without asking questions for over one hour. He only took notes and nodded his head at intervals. When John was done, the Billionaire was silent for five minutes, which to John was an eternity. Clearing his throat, he said, "Young man, you believe many things. You harbour many assumptions. You will have to be here for a couple of days. You are going to unlearn many of your beliefs and reprogramme your mind. Over the years, you have been wrongly wired which is not the fault of yours. You have been exposed to it.

As a matter of fact, all you said, I have heard and it is not in my place to believe or disbelieve them. But, in a couple of days, let's see if you will still have some of these assumptions".

"The fact is that success is something that we all want to attain. It's a station of life that we dream about. Who doesn't want to be successful and powerful? To attain this success in your life, whatever you dream to accomplish, you must realize that to increase your chances, it will all come down to you and the principles you set forth to make your dream a reality'"

"The Billionaire continued. If success were easy, everyone would experience it, but it wouldn't be special whatsoever. Opportunity favours the best prepared. Luck happens when hard work meets opportunity, and success happens when you give it your absolute all".

John Learns The Principle Of Persistence

Unknown to John, the Billionaire and Agnes grew together under the mentorship of Mama Grace.

CHAPTER TWO

John Learns The Principle Of Focus

> *"Successful people maintain a positive focus in life no matter what is going on around them. They stay focused on their past successes rather than their past failures, and on the next action steps they need to take to get them closer to the fulfillment of their goals rather than all the other distractions that life presents to them"*
> *- Jack Canfield*

Immediately after breakfast, the Billionaire sent for John. He arrived and they sat in the study room. He observed that John's confidence level has improved tremendously unlike the first day he met him. He walks with shoulders high and exhumes inner joy. They exchanged pleasantries as John took a seat directly opposite the Billionaire.

"So John, have you been able to learn more things from the books you been reading since you came here"? "Yes Sir", John responded. "The truth of the matter is that had it been I was exposed to these kinds of books early enough, my life would have been different". He continued. "At the university, no effort was made by our lecturers to teach us what we are going to meet in real life. Life is different from all the

What a Billionaire Told a Poor Man

unnecessary theories we were compelled to learn and cram. Most of the subjects are no longer relevant to the highly dynamic society. If you ask me, the school curriculum needs an urgent overhaul.[1]

At home, my parents urged me to read a professional course, come out in flying colours, and get employed. Apparently, they never reasoned that as the population continues to climb, employment opportunities would shrink. At school, the circle goes on. Do you know that throughout my four years sojourn at the university, there was no single day that financial intelligence or entrepreneurship was mentioned? Not even by mistake. We were compelled to continue to consume old and outdated paradigms". [2]

The Billionaire listened with rapt attention. He reasoned that at least John is teachable. He was impressed that some of the books he has read have taken a positive toll on him, besides, he is desirous of changing his narrative.

"John, I am impressed that you have improved. But there are challenges ahead and I advise that you make up your mind to confront them. The journey is far and tortuous. Many have been there and many more are behind, and will still brace the tape when their time comes.

Understanding the right direction and how to get there will help you more than you think. Things are not going to go quickly, in fact, they are going to go slow and take time, but as long as you are moving in the right direction, that's okay. Success is a marathon, not a sprint", the Billionaire stated.

John Learns The Principle Of Focus

"John Benson, what is your vision in life? What is your overall ambition that you are prepared to sacrifice everything to achieve"?

John was speechless as no one has ever asked him such question before.

He thought as he scratches his eye lids while the Billionaire studied him

The Billionaire continued. "Is it that you don't understand the question or your brain cannot manufacture answers to the above question"?

"Okay Sir, let me try. My vision is to be successful in life". "Let me help you further because your answer is vague. At least you know that one day you will die"? "Yes Sir, I know". "You also know that you will not be physically strong at the later part of your life"? "Yes Sir, I am aware". "The question is how would you want to be remembered when you are long gone? Again, when you hear names like Bill Gate, Steve Jobs, King Solomon, Warren Buffet, Aliko Dangote, Jim Ovie, Wright Brothers, Thomas Edison, Albert Einstein, what comes in your mind? You see, the ability or inability to sincerely answer this question will define who you will ever become. People always look outside of themselves to find solutions to their problems. Man is more than the mass of bodies. Man was created to solve all his problems and those he cannot contain with, he should be able to live with them. As a man thinks in his heart, so will he become according to James Allen. The major headache in today's world is that man has become mentally lazy and is not prepared to do his homework. We have appropriated entitlement mentality, believing that the

What a Billionaire Told a Poor Man

government will do everything for us. Many forget that government are run by human beings and are bound to make mistakes. Everybody claims that they love themselves, but no-one is prepared to go the next level. John, if you are asked to climb a high rise building without a staircase or lift. It will be difficult because you don't have wings, but, would not be difficult for birds. But, the moment a ladder is provided, it becomes easy and surmountable. Having a chief goal in life or purpose is the staircase that will catapult you to your chosen destination. Failure to do this, man will be going around in circles"

All these while, John was in deep thought. He tried to think and come to terms with what the Billionaire was talking about, and his experience cannot capture the hidden knowledge that he is trying to put across. The more he tries to figure out what his chief goal is, the more distracted he becomes. Prior to this time, his mind was occupied with how to get a high paying job, solve his immediate financial needs and those around him. He has never thought of being an entrepreneur. All efforts he made in running a small business failed in the past. For him, he was not created to run a business. He believed as he was an employee at the core. The Billionaire allowed the inner turmoil to rage in his mind. John was visibly worried. "But, can entrepreneurship be learnt"? "We need to go on break now to enable you process this information I have given you. This is so important because we cannot go further without knowing where you are headed. Meanwhile, lunch is ready. Use the break period to think".

John Learns The Principle Of Focus

"As a bonus, your chief goal in life should be that aspect of you that you can do without being paid for it. For example, a footballer enjoys playing football even when nobody is watching him. He plays anywhere he sees space. He follows his passion. It is only then that people will notice him and make him a professional.

Also remember that clarity is everything, and understanding what it is you want will bring that to you. It's not a broad idea, it's focused and to the point. By knowing the destination you want to reach, you can continually look at your current path and decide if it's a route that will help you get where you want to go.

Let's meet by 4pm in the library". John was troubled and lost appetite. He was obsessed with how to solve this challenge. He went and sat still but stillness eluded him. Impressions started hitting the window of his mind on a nanosecond basis. Concentration became an illusion. The more he tries to focus, the more thoughts hit his conscious mind.

Suddenly, he remembered that as the only son, his mother taught him how to cook all kinds of delicacies. And, at the age of ten, he cooked sumptuous meal that everybody in the household ate to their satisfaction. John now realized for the first time in life where his strength lies. "I love to cook. I love to see people lick their fingers after eating my food. I like to see satisfied faces each time someone eats my food. The feelings give me joy. In simple language, I love to cook even if am not being paid". But, my greatest challenge now is how to present this to the Billionaire.

What a Billionaire Told a Poor Man

He rushed to the library and unknown to him, the Billionaire was there going through a financial magazine. "Oh, I thought you were resting"? "No Sir", I am looking for plain sheet of paper and pen to enable me to write down my chief goal in life". He collected the materials and dashed out to Room 5. He was elated that John was learning fast. He has a conscious and learning mind. The Billionaire assured himself that the young man would be great if he does not derail from this path he has chosen. Alone in his room, John wrote down countless of chief goals. Earlier, he has read that a goal that is not written down is a wish.

One hour after, he went to present to the Billionaire his chief goal in life. He assured himself that even if what he has written down might not be the best, but the Billionaire would not be disappointed. After all, the Billionaire has consistently said that nobody was born a champion.

John met the Billionaire in the library flipping through the biography of Abraham Lincoln. "How has your day has been going"? "I am fine, Sir". "Have you been able to decipher your chief goal in life"? "Yes Sir". "Is it written down"? "Yes Sir". "Can I have it"? John handed over the piece of paper. The Billionaire studied it and smiled. "Read it out".

"My chief goal in life is to own and run 15 four-star hotels in some major cities of West Africa by 2050" "That is a nice attempt. We will improve it as time goes on. As a matter of fact, this is a good starting point. At least, you have a focus and you attached the time frame to achieve the goal. This is

John Learns The Principle Of Focus

highly commendable. The next stage is how to bring it to the physical equivalent what your mind has created. But, we have had a long day. Let's meet in the study by 8.19am" The Billionaire egressed.

The Billionaire once more wants to find out how meticulous John can be in keeping to time.

Mind operation

The Billionaire had been already in the study room when John came in by 8.16am. "How are you young man"? "I am fine, Sir", John answered. "Nobody can achieve anything worthwhile without having full control of his or her mind. Man is 100 percent mental. It starts from the mind and ends therein. Any kind of creation, man brought to its physical equivalent was first created in the mind. People rarely see what civil engineers do before a building is erected. There is a lot of home work. Most times, it is done mentally".

In his book, 'The Science of Getting Rich', Wallace Wattles gave these postulations.

> "There is a thinking stuff from which all things are made, and which, in its original state permeates, penetrates, and fills the interspaces of the universe.
>
> A thought, in this substance, produces the thing that is imaged by the thought.
>
> Man can form things in his thought, and by impressing his thought upon formless substance, can cause the thing he thinks about to be created".

What a Billionaire Told a Poor Man

"There is a thinking stuff from which all things are made,
and which, in its original state permeates,
penetrates, and fills the interspaces of the universe.
A thought, in this substance,
produces the thing that is imaged by the thought.
Man can form things in his thought,
and by impressing his thought upon formless substance,
can cause the thing he thinks about to be created".

I recommended that you read these statements several times until you accept them as truth. Make these statements part of you. Believe them as you believe the law of gravity and electricity.

"John, hear me today. Let me repeat myself for emphasis sake. Read the above statements several times until it becomes part of you. Memorize it. Reduce it on a post card and carry it anywhere you go. Take it as a spiritual creed. Do not allow anybody to discourage you about the hidden truths and power these statements contain. And do go to any place where there will be an argument about the efficacy of these postulations. They have the capacity to change your inner being".

"Last week some people came here for employment, I asked one of them to point the position of the mind on his body. To my shock, he pointed to the chest region. You see, if you do not know where the mind is on your body, how could you possibly deploy it for use"? He continued. "Man has one mind, but divided into two -the conscious mind,

John Learns The Principle Of Focus

and subconscious mind. Both must work together to achieve any set objective. None can work in isolation.

Unfortunately the more powerful of the two minds is the subconscious, but the least used. Many are contented with the five objective senses and relegating to the other mind to background.

The conscious mind is that aspect of the mind that hears, feels, sees, tastes and smells-the five objective senses.

The subconscious mind is the powerhouse that creates. It can enslave us or empower us. It can plunge us into the depth of misery or take heights of ecstasy. I urge you to read every available literature you can get on this subject.

What has happened prior to this time is that you have not learned how to make use of the subconscious mind. Shortly, I assure you, you will see clearer pictures the moment you learn how. The Billionaire continued, "Since, you have made up your mind regarding your chief goal in life, you must at once begin to see yourself as the owner of a chain of hotels. You must affirm it daily and visualize yourself running those hotels via your subconscious mind. If you believe, you can. More so, you must take massive action.

The subconscious mind is the workshop of the human mind. It is where the real job is done. It is the picturing power of the mind, the formation of the mental images, pictures, or mental representation of objects or ideas.

This is the reason why I have taken the time to teach you the importance of not using your mind

What a Billionaire Told a Poor Man

negatively. Produce the film in your mind. That thriller, the person you want to be in the future. Start watching the film daily. It does not hurt. Young man, what you must understand, and accept forever is that words are powerful.

These words can be written or spoken, never allow anybody to lower your self-esteem through negative utterances against your person.

If, for example, someone told you that, you will never amount to anything; your conscious mind will filter this statement and let you realize that the person is just speaking from this figment of his/her imaginations.

Remember how you felt when you were accused of stealing $1000 of which you never knew anything about. Apparently, you felt low and wanted to die. It is possible that scenario culminated in your looking at the Lagoon as an option. I don't think that you would forget in a hurry at the security post few hours ago. They were mere words. Adamu did not hit with any object, but you fainted. This goes to tell you how powerful words could be".

"Be religious in telling yourself positive things. Many have had accidents because they received bad news while driving. Then, if bad news affects both the mind and the body, so will good news do the same. Affirmations are what will keep you going along the long journey. It's the positive mindset of "I'm going to make this happen." It's instilling belief in yourself. With affirmations, you are defining your own reality. By transmitting this positive energy into the universe, it eventually manifests into reality. As your mind

John Learns The Principle Of Focus

adopts this view, it helps shape the world around you to fit in".

The Billionaire continued. "Don't mind your station in life at the moment. The subconscious mind is like a robot. It can be tricked. It does not know the difference real and imagined. It carries out instructions from the conscious mind. That's why you should be careful with the words you use. You must have heard that faith cometh by hearing. You must be religious in telling yourself all the nice things. I advise that you mentally produce a-one-minute-commercial of John Benson. This mental tape must be played at least twice a day- prior before you sleep-when you are in the drowsy state and upon waking up. Make this tape as interesting as possible. Laugh as you mentally play this tape. Mentally see self in a big screen while the tape is being played. See people cheering you as if it is in real life. If done regularly, the subconscious mind will move to, work and does the rest".

"John, there is an affirmation that Emile Coue gave the world. History had it that he used the affirmation to cure cancer patients. It will only be effective if you believe.

It is-'Day by day, in every way, I am getting better and better'. It is this simple but powerful. There is power in simplicity, and it is the reason why many don't believe the secrets of wealth building because it is always simple.

However, Napoleon Hill paraphrased Coue's statement to- 'Day by day, in every way, I am becoming more successful'. Make it your daily menu.

What a Billionaire Told a Poor Man

Recite this at least 300 times daily and see how powerful words can be.

Understanding self

"From my over seven decades sojourn here, the Billionaire continued, "I have come to the realization that most people you see on the street are oblivious of who they are. Very few take the time to study who they are, their strengths and weaknesses.

The human brain is a complex machine. It is capable of doing any task given to it.

Even the Psalmist questioned who man is that the Creator is mindful of him. He also sent His only Son to visit him, according to the Holy Bible. The earlier you understand that you are fearfully and wonderfully made, the better for you".

The Billionaire went further, "John, at least you remember that the philosophers of the old admonished man to know thyself". It is only when you know thyself that you can make meaningful and sustainable progress.

Young man, I join the sages of the old the request that you know thyself.

Let's go for lunch as the table has been set. We will talk again by tomorrow.

CHAPTER 3

John Learns The Principle Of Discipline

> *"You need three things to win: discipline, hard work and, before everything maybe, commitment. No one will make it without those three. Sport teaches you that"*- Haile Gebrselassie

John did not sleep, perhaps because of loads training, he is undergoing from the Billionaire's feet, coupled with the fact that he will be going for an errand.

The PA had intimated him last night he would be going to Victoria Island-Lagos to collect a cheque from one of the most difficult customers of the Billionaire. He was duly informed that the client is a good client, but difficult to handle.

This was a classic example of an irritant. Like it is said, customers are kings. The Billionaire would have done away with him, but for the fact that he has learned how to handle troublesome clients

What made John curious was that the Billionaire never spoke to him about the client. Hence, his options are limited. The task must be accomplished.

What a Billionaire Told a Poor Man

Around 10am, John was seated at the cozy office of the client. The environment was serene, laced with ambience depicting of officialdom. The reception was small but inviting.

Exchanging pleasantries with the secretary, he waited for his turn to see the much talked about client.

For over four hours, he waited. Intermittently, he prompted the secretary to remind her boss that he was still waiting. But, the secretary retorted that it would not be any need since the form he filled is still with her Boss

"My dear, my Boss will call you when he is ready to see you. No one has ever succeeded in bullying my boss", the secretary quipped.

A few minutes after, John was asked to go in. On sighting him, the client started shouting at the tip of his voice.

"Yes! Who sent you? What do you want? Must you see me physically"? Tons of questions at the same time, John was calm and refused to be intimidated. He genuflected but humbly and respectfully told the client that he was sent by Chief Godfrey to collect a cheque.

On hearing this, the client lost his cool and started charging aggressively. John just stood his grounds apparently because; he has been warned coupled with the fact that it is a litmus test for him enroute his mentor-ship with the Billionaire.

But, when the client saw that John was not jittery, he asked him the value of the cheque that he wants to collect. John did not waste time to mention the figure. The client was impressed with the calmness of John

John Learns The Principle Of Discipline

and quickly instructed the accountant to issue cheque in favour of Chief Godfrey.

Mission accomplished. He was elated that his first assignment was executed successfully.

On arrival, the Billionaire instructed John to meet him in his study room. The Billionaire was already seated when John stepped in. Waved him to a seat, the Billionaire continued romance his Apple laptop.

Shortly, he shut down the system, and asked John if he collected the cheque. The Billionaire nodded and never wanted details regarding what transpired in the client's office. For him, the most important thing is the result.

The Billionaire asks John to go for a short rest and come back by 5pm.

As usual, John was in the study chamber on time. He greeted the Billionaire and sat down. "Young man, you see in life, it does not matter if you are intelligent or talented, but there is a quality one must possess and failure to learn it will only spell doom.

Most people you meet on the street are not disciplined, they are not patient. They make promises to both themselves, others and break them without berthing an eye lid.

Discipline is the only oil with which the machine of success pivots. Challenges will come and it is the only discipline that can serve as a dependable partner. When things are falling like a pack of cards, discipline gathers.

I sent you to my client's office. I knew that he was going to shout, delay you and shop for excuses not to honour his obligations. He could not find excuses

What a Billionaire Told a Poor Man

because you were unperturbed in the face of unnecessary ranting. Many people you see on the streets are carrying burdens and they are looking for where they can offload their miseries. Your number one assignment is to make sure that nobody uses you as a dumping arena".

"Have you ever heard of "New year Resolution"? "Yes Sir", John answered. "But have you ever asked why people do not always obey their own instructions"? "No Sir". "Discipline is the key- they lack discipline.

In the course of my dealings with the sons and daughters of men, I have come to realize that no man controls others unless he first controls himself. There is a saying that 'whom the gods would destroy, they first make mad'. What you must understand fully is that no man can rise to fame and a huge fortune without carrying others along with him. It simply cannot be done".

John was listening with rapt attention. The Billionaire went on, "One of the major causes of misfortune, loss of business, divorce, strife, bickering, and wars is that majority of the people are not disciplined or do not have self-control. I wonder what any man can achieve no matter his station in society without discipline".

"Sometime last year, I went to an area of Lagos with my driver. The driver made a turn at a wrong place. Traffic officials arrested us and took us to their station. Ordinarily, a normal person would have shouted or argued with them. At the station, I demanded to see their boss. When I met him, I calmly explained my predicament and pleaded guilty. And because I was

John Learns The Principle Of Discipline

humble, he gave us a light ticket.

In my office, I hung a frame, with this inscription "Don't do the natural thing". Each time somebody comes to my office for the first time, he/she always ask what message the frame conveys. I always tell them that doing the natural thing is like; if you slap me and I will in turn slap you. That's the natural thing. Turning the next cheek is the unnatural thing, and nothing disarms an adversary than turning the other cheek.

The world will be a better place if majority learn how not to do the natural". At this point, John wanted to start taking notes, but the Billionaire stopped him.

"Young man, taking notes is good. But, many times, we don't usually find time to review our notes. For now, concentrate in internalizing the concepts therein, and it will bear fruit later.

No man can be successful without discipline. Every day, people come here shouting at the tip of their voices with all kinds of complaints. These are your customers. It is widely believed that customers are hard to please. It might be true to a large extent. But, with discipline or self-control, it can be conquered. People want to be helped. I don't understand why any businessman should be rude".

"In my neighbourhood, one young boy inherited a huge sum of money from his parents. He became rude to anybody that disagrees with him. He took to alcohol and some expensive life style. He bought vehicles that consume so much gasoline.

On one occasion, he came here to seek for advice on investment. He bragged how much that is in his

What a Billionaire Told a Poor Man

possession. But, what he forgot that he has never made money on his own. He ran into money. You remember that man in the Bible that came to Jesus and asked what he will do to inherit the kingdom of heaven"? "Yes, I do" "Jesus told him to go and sell his belongings and follow Him. It was recorded that the man went away sorrowfully.

It was at this point that Jesus said that it is easier for a Carmel to pass through the eye of a needle than for the rich man to enter heaven".

As if copying from Jesus, I asked him to reduce his expensive lifestyle. Sell off those heavy duty vehicles. Reduce alcohol intake. Buy some books on financial intelligence and enroll in some self-control programmes.

I told him after he must have done all these; he should come back for a more detailed discussion. Just as the rich man in the Bible, he left me sorrowful.

Months after, I learnt that he was building a restaurant. I giggled within myself, because I am sure that he does not have the temperament to handle customers. "John, the restaurant business is a serious business. People are careful where they eat. The moment the owner is given to careless life style, customers will cease from patronizing the place.

Besides, exuberance has fully taken hold of him. Many times, I have seen him quarreling with would-be customers. When he finally finished building the restaurant, all and sundry were called for the opening ceremony. I never needed a soothsayer to tell me that the restaurant would be a failed business. The young man lacked discipline and self- control. He exchanges

John Learns The Principle Of Discipline

hot arguments with almost all the customers".

Just as Dale Carnegie in his classic, "How to Win Friends and Influence People, advised mankind never to engage in an unnecessary argument.

According to him, "nobody can win arguments. Even if you are able to amass all, the entire logic in this world, you are also a loser. This is because the other person will feel bad when you must have gone".

"True to type, the last time, I passed through the location of the restaurant, it has been closed down.

John, I am emphasizing on discipline or self-control because he who understands it, cannot walk a lonely road.

You must owe it to yourself never allow emotions to stand on your way to success. People rarely forgive unguarded utterances, guard your mouth, once, it goes out, it is impossible to get it back. You must have noted that any disciplined person does not engage in frivolous tendencies, greed, avarice or hatred. The person is always contented with the little or much the Cosmic has allowed him to possess.

A disciplined person will never under any circumstances spread rumors against the next person or seek revenge or cause harm.

They are happy people and always enthusiastic about the outcome of the events. They are always expectant of positive results.

John, I am going to give you an assignment. Talk is cheap. We can only learn by putting what we learnt into practice".

John, the Billionaire continued, "If you are observant, there is a small flowing Lake a stone-throw from here.

What a Billionaire Told a Poor Man

Have you ever noticed it", John nodded in affirmation.

"In the next sixty days and by 6am, pick up a stone from that heap of granite and throw it in. And, by 5pm, pick another and do likewise. Do this for 60 days.

This might be elementary to you. It may look so foolish to you. But, that's the assignment. By the end of 60 days, we will talk about it.

You know, the total numbers of stones you are going to throw inside the Lake are 120? John nodded. But, it will negate the essence by trying to throw all at the same time or throw in two once as against going two times in a day".

He kept wondering the direction that Billionaire is headed. "You see; one thing is certain, don't ever contemplate to cheat the process. Unknown to you, I have an in-built mechanism to ascertain how religious you are going carry out this assignment. Besides, there would not be any excuse whatsoever. None would be acceptable. No matter the circumstances or situation. No matter how inclement the weather is, the assignment must be accomplished twice daily".

Suddenly the Billionaire looked at the wall clock and screamed ah! We have been talking for a long time. It is almost time for dinner. As usual, he pressed the bell and the PA appeared with a speed of light.

Kindly instruct the kitchen to get dinner for two. As the Billionaire was talking with the PA, John was engulfed in deep thought. He wondered why an adult would be throwing ordinary stone twice a day and for a whole 60 days. What is this eccentric Billionaire up

John Learns The Principle Of Discipline

to, he queried. Without readily available answers, the Billionaire nudged him to a wakeful state.

"I know that you are thinking about"- why an adult would be doing with throwing stones in the Lake. That was exactly what my benefactor instructed me years ago to do. I am happy that I did as instructed. At times, in this wonderful planet, we do not get answers to all our queries and, this is one of them. It is not scientific. But, the aspect that baffled me when I did mine was that you can't cheat the process. By the time you start tomorrow, you will come to the realization that this assignment is cheat proof. No one can cheat the process.

However, it was the greatest undertaking in my life. "Let me warn you, the system recognizes the time you picked the stone and the time you dropped it. It will be fun as the days go by".

Farm experience

Meanwhile, after your morning ritual tomorrow, you will accompany me to the farm. We will be leaving by 7am, the Billionaire ordered".

The Billionaire has a-one-hundred-hectare-farm-land at Agbara, Ogun State. Prior to this visit, John has never seen that kind of large expanse of land before. All kinds of agriculture go on there.

The farm manager was handy to receive them. The Billionaire wants to teach John that life requires patience and endurance. "You must always put your eyes on the crown at all times".

He took John to the poultry section where he brought

What a Billionaire Told a Poor Man

out a day-old-chick. "You see, after sometimes, this day-old would grow to a full chicken. There is nothing you can do to cheat the growing up process. Nature must take its course. The problem of human beings is that they think they are smart. It is only those that align with the laws of the nature that will be able to build real and sustainable wealth. Anything to the contrary, is tantamount to the building a high scrapper on a shallow foundation. To nurture and grow a business, the entrepreneur must have the heart of a hunter or a farmer.

After romancing with the day-old for a couple of minutes, he took John to the garden section. He picked pumpkin seedling and caressed it, and said "unless the seed dies, it will not produce its kind. The law stipulates that it must be planted in a fertile soil, and on a friendly temperature.

You remember the Parable of the Sower as told in the Bible? Nothing can be truer than that. Each time I see people misbehave on the street; I remember the parable and move on.

It is your job to make your mind fertile, plant good principles and in due time, just as this healthy seedling, it will produce its kinds.

If you are observant, I have taken so much time to dwell on the importance of the discipline and self-control. You must promise yourself that you must keep all the promises made to yourself and others".

"Discipline is so central to a man's life solely because it is the Ombudsman. It is an unseen guide. Once you have taken any assignment, distraction must come. It is only disciplined that will propel you to see the end

John Learns The Principle Of Discipline

of the assignment; you must not take lightly the habit of reading books. What books are to the mind, is what food is to the body. In my experience, most successful businessmen I have contact with had large libraries. Reading must be your second nature.

It puts you ahead of competition. It builds your mind. It makes you analyze issues from the point of knowledge.

Above all, each field of human endeavours has its vocabulary. Any field you have chosen to play, you must speak the language and it is only books that will take you there. Always read economics and history books. Let's go now; it is getting late", the Billionaire said.

On their way home, the Billionaire branched to one of his hotels, which government authorities have classified as a 4-star hotel.

He has never told John that he owns a chain of hotels, and not even when John chose owning and running a chain of hotels as his chief goal in life.

The Billionaire has a permanent suite where no guess is allowed to stay. He was quickly ushered into an extravagantly furnished room with plenty of headroom and space. The sofa was of Italian origin with a gold plated water bed. The dressing mirror was lined with diamond with its floor dotted with Spanish marbles.

The walls are dotted with paintings of Leonardo DI ser Piero DA Vinci and Michelangelo Mersida Caraaggio.

The Billionaire ordered for lunch for two and said nothing about the ownership of the place. But the

What a Billionaire Told a Poor Man

level of compliments bestowed on the Billionaire suggested one thing. It is either he is the owner of the hotel or a regular visitor. But, he did not want to ask. He has learned early enough how to mind his business.

John told the Billionaire that the hotel is the type he would want to build when he starts his hotel business.

"If you can see it, you can as well own it. Be disciplined and every other thing would be added unto you.

Shortly after, they left for Banana Island. Remember your ritual, this evening, as he alighted from the vehicle.

"One more thing, I have a couple of books on Emotional Intelligence. Peruse some of them as the knowledge will sharpen your skills on the importance of self-discipline.

Let's meet by 5:16am. John thought deeply why the Billionaire chose 5:16am when ordinary mortals are still enjoying sleep. He, however, set his alarm clock at 4:30am as he has imbibed punctuality as a way of life.

CHAPTER FOUR

John Learns The Principle Of Integrity

> *"The supreme quality for leadership is unquestionably integrity. Without it, no real success is possible, no matter whether it is on a section gang, a football field, in an army, or in an office"-Dwight D. Eisenhower*

John met the Billionaire the next day in the study room as agreed. But contrary to the aura of happiness that the Billionaire always exhumes, he was a little bit pensive. He seems worried and distant.

John wanted to find out what the issue was, but the Billionaire dismissed his queries with a wave of the hand. Continuing, "John, one of the most important virtues any businessman should possess is integrity".

The Billionaire continued. "A philosopher once said that if honesty did not exist, someone would invent it as the best way of getting rich. Young man, human beings are nothing without integrity. People all over the world are looking for those they can transact with, those who would not change the goal post in the middle of the game.

As a matter of fact, I have devised a way of testing the

What a Billionaire Told a Poor Man

integrity of people I am going into business relationship with; I always insist that we play golf. And, if they don't, play golf, we must play any kind of game. This is because, if such a person can cheat in something as elementary as golf, they will still cheat in the arena of business. The moment I notice it, I will call it quits, and nothing can sway me to do otherwise".

Let me give you an example: one of the leading automobile dealers in Nigeria imported vehicles at the exchange rate of N160 to one dollar. But, when the payment was due, the dollar has skyrocketed to N480 to a dollar.

Ordinarily, he would have gone to his partners to re-negotiate. But, he never did. He chose to bear his losses. This singular act of honouring the agreement endeared him to his partners and in-turn, they made him the sole distributor of their brand in West Africa. This is how integrity works. It open doors and unlocks already shut ones.

"It is important that you learn this principle and commit it to heart. If you don't, people will eventually find out and you will be out of business.

Capital has never been in short supply to the man of integrity. They control the purse of men of means.

There are many out there looking for who they can partner with and create value for the benefit of all concerned. But, the fear that the capital might not be returned makes them not to invest,

If you conduct a survey in the financial institutions, there are so much idle funds unutilized at the vaults of commercial banks. The owners of these funds are willing to invest in businesses only and only if there are

John Learns The Principle Of Integrity

guarantees of return of investment".
It dawned on John that he only went to school to acquire book knowledge. The Billionaire went on with his lectures. "We are currently living in changing times. People are in a hurry to be rich. The rat race has piqued many people in dangerous situations. The truth is that businesses cannot sail smoothly without credit. To that man who is conscious of his words, and does everything within his power to live by his words, the sky is his starting point.

The Billionaire tests John

The next day, the Billionaire sent John to the bank to make a cash deposit. Deliberately, John was given N100, 000 over what he was to pay in. Noticing the overage, John laughed and assured himself that taking what is not his own has never been his life style. When he came back, he reported to the Billionaire that the money was over by N100, 000 and he pretended that he never knew about it. He, however, thanked John for his honesty and thoroughness.

"This scenario got John thinking. Does it mean that the Billionaire made a mistake or that it was a deliberate ploy to test his honesty"? "No matter what his intentions were, I have returned the money that does not belong to me". Realizing that John was thinking about what transpired in the bank, he pointed out to John that being reliable is another virtue that anybody who wants to be rich must inculcate. "Many people take many things for granted. When your customers come to realize that

What a Billionaire Told a Poor Man

you are reliable, you will never lack clients. The essence of investing in business is to maximize profits. And, it can only be done if you have been able to build an army of clientele base.
Guaranteeing a repeat business is now dependent on your ability to make clients to trust you".
You see, every business, no matter how small or big stands on four legs:-

Customers
Employers
Suppliers
Financiers.

All the four legs must be in alignment, the table is bound to fall should any of the legs is broken, and none is more important than the other. Create time to study these concepts and I have a couple of books in the library that treat these concepts extensively.

Getting Capital

"Anybody you meet on the street will readily tell you that his/her greatest impediment to go into business is capital. But, I don't think so. Few people know what they want when money comes to them suddenly.
Is it any wonder that only 2 percent of lottery winners retire rich? Many have inherited wealth or married rich wives. For them, the problem was not capital, but how to manage it. What has kept many down is not capital but ideas or channels that the money would be deployed to, once it is within reach.
From my experience, what most people do is that they

John Learns The Principle Of Integrity

wait till they get capital before they commence plans on how to spend the money.

John, this is a wrong approach and must be avoided just as you would run away from a rattlesnake".

People of means will not give their hard earned money if you don't have an already tested plan on how to spend it. This is one of the reasons why banks in Nigeria do not fund startups.

When you start that which you are convinced and knowledgeable about, investors will fund your experience. Every business has its lower side. It is only when you have mastered the industry you are interested in and done serious homework that capital will flow in.

Without a definite plan, it is not likely that you will attract capital.

Again, once you have acquired capital, there must be clear-cut plans on how to pay back, ability to pay back as an when due, is the only talisman that unlocks the pockets of the rich men. The chief work of commercial banks is to fund businesses.

Any man that has acquired the onerous discipline to pay back even when the odds don't favour him cannot lack capital. People will always want extra money. Position yourself solidly with the skill of paying as an when due and capital will become your slave".

You must learn to ask

The Billionaire continued. "Just as it is said in advertising, unless, you say I am here, nobody will notice you. You must learn how to ask. You don't

What a Billionaire Told a Poor Man

know who will say yes or no unless you ask. People seldom ask. It is either they are ashamed to ask or they are afraid that they would be turned down. As a businessman, it does not matter. You must ask. You make a move by asking. No matter what you know, unless you take action, the talent will die within you.

I know a young man who secured a small contract to supply 930 bottles of cooking gas to a chain of hotels in Lagos State. He does not have the money to do the supply, and banks were not ready to fund the transaction. His only hope was to ask relations and friends for assistance and share profits with them. He refused to take action and the Local Purchase Order (LPO) expired and the contract was cancelled.

It is my belief that you take this principle seriously. One day, you will be in a situation even if you have so much, and your business might need partners to expand to other frontiers. Even banks borrow money from sister banks to fund large transactions.

If you must move to the next level, you must learn how to ask", the Billionaire concluded.

CHAPTER 5
John Learns The Principle Of Savings

> *"In the absence of the gold standard, there is no way to protect savings from confiscation through inflation. There is no safe store of value"- Alan Greenspan*

The Billionaire took John to the Lake where he throws stones twice a day. They sat ashore and watched the blueness of the Lake.
"Young man, have you ever noticed most Lakes don't flow"? "Yes Sir" John answered. "Nature is wonderful. This particular one flows. It is a wonder. It was the attraction why I bought this place. It was strange but pleasing to my eyes.
For this Lake to continue to flow, it must have a constant supply, otherwise, after sometime, it will dry off. The source will also have another source. That is how nature has made it. We can only cooperate with her. Our options are limited really".
"For sure, almost everybody has made money at one time or the other. From my experience, the sons and daughters of men hate to save money. According to them, they are not earning enough to set a part aside.

What a Billionaire Told a Poor Man

I have argued strongly that it is not natural to save money. It is alien to man. It is made more difficult because man is transient. We are here on a journey. Many do not see need to deny themselves some monetary pleasure, for the greater goal ahead.

Habit formation

The habit of saving is not what one can wish for. Just like any other habit, it takes time to be internalized. One of the greatest authorities in the art of saving money is George Clason. In his book, 'The Richest Man in Babylon', he argued powerfully that a part not less than 10 percent must be saved from all earnings.
According to Clason, failure to do this will lead to poverty in future. He argued that if 10 percent is saved over time, the saver would be rich if he learns the art of investment.
"Let me warn you! Many have argued that saving money will never make you rich. But, what they did not capture is that the saved money must be deployed to investment windows that will consistently generate income.
I agree with them that keeping money in a savings account will never make anyone rich".
"You see, most Nigerian banks give a paltry interest rate of 2 percent on savings account per annum. But the inflation is at 18.6 percent as of today. It is obvious that savers are losers. What this means is that the saved money will continue to lose value. Let me illustrate. "A man fell inside a soak away and started shouting fire! Fire! The neighbours gathered and

John Learns The Principle Of Savings

called in the fire fighters. When they arrived, they could not dictate any sign of fire. The man inside the pit became more hysterical and increased in pitch, fire! Fire! The fire operators finally located him and pulled him out. "Brethren, why were you calling 'fire, fire', when there was no fire?" And he retorted, "had it been I was shouting 'shit! shit,' would you have come?

"John, we must save smart, putting money aside is just the first leg of the arithmetic. The second and the most important leg is that the saved money must be invested.

Also, you must at all times avoid buying anything that you did not plan to buy. No matter the pressure from the sales people should not sway you. Always ignore them".

Everybody must have a budget. Once it is not in your budget, gently tell them that you have overshot your monthly budget. Don't say more than that".

"You must have also heard that investment is risky. Yes it is if you don't do your homework well before deploying your saved funds to ventures that you don't understand. It is only then that it becomes risky. Scammers will come with sweet-coated tongues. They will promise you high yields.

Ask them to give you time to investigate. It is always important to check the background of those introducing deals to you.

By all means check them out. Unfortunately, their proposals come in complex matrices. Don't fool yourself. Be humble by asking those that are knowledgeable. You cannot ask informed questions, if you don't know what to ask. Always seek the advice

What a Billionaire Told a Poor Man

of your bankers and those doing well in the industry that you are interested in. Most rich men are eager to tell their stories. Make friends with them, they are always ready to talk. Buy them lunch and gifts. Learn from them. This is important to enable you to avoid the mistakes they made when they were building their financial empire".

Don't forget also that there are fake local purchase orders issued in connivance with some unscrupulous members of staff. Always check.

There is what they call blue chip companies. Make it as a rule to transact with such companies. Always confirm the signatures on the LPO. Generating income is not a tea party affair. Once money is in your pocket, you must take stringent steps to secure it".

Money lending

The Billionaire sipped some water and continued. "People are always looking for money. The society has been commercialized that man needs money to survive. No man can live to his full potential without money. You can't own or show love to someone without the bestowal of gifts. Money is central in our lives. Anybody can philosophize about the need for an austere lifestyle. But, man needs food and water to keep the body system running.

Every day, people throng my office asking for handouts and all kinds of business proposals. I created a system that directs them to my accountant who will in turn ask relevant questions to ascertain if the business is viable or not.

John Learns The Principle Of Savings

They may come in with flowery languages, cars and expensive clothes, just to give you the impression that all is well. They go as far as taking you to lunch and spend lavishly. John, be careful. It is a game. Seek the advice of an expert.

Any unsecured loan is money gone too far. Do everything within the legal umbrella to secure your money. You see, money is like petrol. No matter how expensive the car maybe, if there is no gasoline, it becomes a toy".

John has learnt so much from the Billionaire that he is looking for opportunities to put into practice what he has learnt for the past eight months. Billionaire assured him that he should not be in a hurry. "Time will come when the master will no longer be available. For now, your preoccupation should be continuous acquisition of these principles on how to navigate sharks infested Business Ocean".

CHAPTER 6
John Learns The Principle Of Gratitude

> *"Gratitude unlocks the fullness of life. It turns what we have into enough, and more. It turns denial into acceptance, chaos to order, confusion to clarity. It can turn a meal into a feast, a house into a home, a stranger into a friend"- Melody Beattie*

The next day, the Billionaire took John to Ikorodu town, a suburb near Lagos, to meet an elderly man. On their way they entered a Super Mart where the Billionaire made extravagant purchases. The car booth was loaded with all kinds of wines, spirits, beverages, cereals and toiletries.

The elderly man, perhaps in his 80's was glad to receive the Billionaire, who he fondly calls 'G.O'.

"Oh 'G.O', you never told me that you were coming to see me. I hope all is well"?

The Billionaire retorted, "My King, when has it become a crime to pay homage to a traditional ruler"? Both laughed and hugged each other.

The King served them fresh palm wine and fruits. Both talked about old times and challenges they faced together.

What a Billionaire Told a Poor Man

The Billionaire reiterated that he is still very grateful for assisting him to buy the 100 hectares of land in his domain despite fierce resistance from his cabinet members and subjects. The tussle lasted for over two years and at the end, the Billionaire won the case and was asked to compensate the inhabitants which he happily did.

Henceforth, peace reigned. That is where the Billionaire situated his farm. The Billionaire gave John instructions and with the help of the King's servants, the booth was offloaded to the delight of the King. He was lavish in thanking the Billionaire that despite that peace has reigned, he still remembers to say thank you. "May the god of my Ancestors bless and reward you handsomely. From where you have gotten the money to buy all these for me, may Allah in his Infinite Mercy replace and replenish you bountifully", the King prayed.

Before, they left for Banana Island, the Billionaire handed a fat envelope to the King.

"John, again, you must learn to say thank you when one does you a favour. Everybody appreciates it. Even from the scriptures, many examples abound where the creator himself relished in thanksgiving"

He continued. "Appreciate what you've achieved so far, and see that what you want and where you're going, are not what you need or what you must do. Rather, these are things and actions that will make your situation even better. Being thankful and grateful will change your life dramatically"

"Remember that before Jesus performs any

John Learns The Principle Of Gratitude

miracle, He always gives thanks to His Father. Gratitude is the invisible wire that draws more blessings from the Inexhaustible Source. It has never failed to connect. Also, when Jesus healed the ten lepers, only one returned to say thank you. Jesus took notice and blessed him more abundantly.

The man we went to see was instrumental to my acquiring the land where I built my farm. The resistance was huge. The indigenes became envious and did so much to prevent my acquisition.

But this man, stood by me. He made sure that his people did not dispossess me of what I have duly paid for.

So, from time to time, I have always come here to say thank you. The imbroglio was so fierce that his people nearly banished him. Still, he never betrayed me. I am extremely grateful to him".

"John, please as a rule, always do this. Imbibe a grateful mind. In the place of work, praise your workers, feed their self-esteem. In the family praise your wife. It is a psychological truth that human beings are not beings of logic but emotion.

The sons and daughters of men will forget those who offend them, but will not forget those who lower their self-esteem.

Young man, God loves appreciation and thanksgiving. Man and woman love appreciation, even animals are not left out.

Understand this and practice it, it will take you to the next level". At this point, John was gradually getting agitated. The way the Billionaire has

What a Billionaire Told a Poor Man

addressed him of late gives the impression as if he is already an owner of a business.

The Billionaire has been telling me things as if I am his partner. But, I am just here obeying instructions from him, John said mentally.

As if he read his mind, the Billionaire calmed him down. "But don't worry son, time is fast coming when all you have learnt would be put to test. It is almost here.

Moreover, teamwork is essential in sustaining any business venture. You can't possibly work alone. Perhaps, when you start any enterprise, make sure that you hire the best hands.

Each person has areas of strengths and weaknesses. It will be your job to hire people who will compliment your areas of weakness and build a formidable team. Never hire anyone out of sympathy or sentiment, or because the person is related to you.

Business is business. The essence of business is business. Sentiments should be at all times relegated to the back seat as it does not have any place in building business systems.

Again, cooperation is one word you should not play with. No matter what you sell, you need people to buy from you. You must live a life where people see you as somebody who is helping them.

Solve their challenges. You must be ready to advance anybody that comes in contact with you. Even if you have the best product in the world, with a poor attitude, people will find an alternative.

John Learns The Principle Of Gratitude

Nature hates monopoly. Nature is lavish. There is abundance to that man who can see. Learn to listen to your clients. They came to you to solve their problems. Never refer them to your subordinates what you can solve. If you must do that, personally take them to who will solve their challenge and give express orders. Always make personal touch as a rule".

Just as Dale Carnegie told his audience that "the feeling of importance is what everybody wants". He went ahead to say that "many have gone insane in their quest to feel important".

"You see, somebody's toothache is more important to him than an earthquake in a neighbouring country. People love to be pampered. When they come crying, empathize with them. Calm their nerves. Just like a child would rush to her mother to show his wound to earn sympathy. We are all children at the core. The ability to manage human beings is a skill you cannot delegate".

As the Billionaire continues to speak in this manner, John begins to get more agitated. "I have learnt a lot from the Billionaire. I am eager to tell the world that the John has changed. I need to see Ambrose. Despite that both of us made second class upper, we did not learn so much regarding how businesses are run, he thought.

Reading his mind once again, the Billionaire interrupted John's flow of thoughts. "I will schedule one of these days to enable you meet with some of your old friends. You have been here now for over one year. Before long, I will go to the way of all flesh".

What a Billionaire Told a Poor Man

On hearing these words, John rebuked the Billionaire.

CHAPTER 7

John Learns The Principle Of Marketing

"I have always said that everyone is in sales. Maybe you don't hold the title of a salesperson, but if the business you are in requires you to deal with people, you, my friend, are in sales"
- Zig Ziglar

Being a Trader

As John entered his room, he was agitated that the Billionaire was speaking in parables of late. It gave him grave concern. But the Billionaire never betrayed any negative emotion. But a close observation will depict that all is not well with him. He was still in deep thought when his phone rang. Picking it up, the Billionaire was on the other end, "John, please come to my study". The Billionaire was pacing the floor when John entered. "Sir, I hope that you are fine"? "Oh yes. Just that there are many things I need to sort out before I go". "Where are you going to? Can I accompany you"? "No John. That would not be

What a Billionaire Told a Poor Man

necessary. I still have a couple of months to be here. Never mind. I just pray that I will be able to stay before then". Once again, the Billionaire puts John on another round of mental encounter. "Anyway, I called for an important discussion. John free your mind at least for now, I am still with you. John, are you a trader the Billionaire asked"? "No, sir, I am not. Like I told you the last time, my overall ambition is to run a chain of hotels in strategic locations in West Africa". "That is ok". The Billionaire continued. "Assuming you have a couple of hotels now, how do you intend to bring in clients to visit your hotel? John thought for a moment, but kept silent, the Billionaire probed. Just think a little. The human brain is equipped to solve almost all problems and challenges. The problem with most people is that they rarely think. I agree that thinking is the hardest job anyone can undertake. However, you must learn how to set aside a couple of minutes daily to think. It is imperative if you are serious regarding running a chain of hotels". "Honestly, I have not thought about it", John said. "But John, you made second class upper division at the university, what is difficult in attempting to answer a question? You are afraid that you might not get the right answer? Remember that it is not an examination". "Just try," the Billionaire encouraged him. "Well, I will advertise", John responded. "Good, that is fine. You see, all of us are traders. The only difference is that many are not conscious of it. At any giving time, we are selling something. It might be goods or services, tangible or intangible products. But, is Bill Gate a trader"? "No, sir, he is not, he is a

John Learns The Principle Of Marketing

computer engineer and founder of Microsoft", John stated. You are right, the Billionaire said, "but what does he do with the software after manufacturing them"? John became silent as he thought harder. As if by flash on the side of him, he began to have a fair idea where the Billionaire was headed. "Sir, I think, I am getting a clearer picture of what you are saying. Please tell me", the Billionaire pleaded

"What you mean is that no matter what we do, we must let people know about it. As a future owner of hotels, I must come up with a strategy to make people come to my hotels", John pointed out. "You have gotten the entire picture, the Billionaire continued. "Not letting people know what you do is tantamount to lighting a lamp and hiding it inside a cupboard. The major hurdle is to accept that you are a trader because you are selling a service. Your clients come in daily to buy your services. Any day you don't have anything to sell, they will stop coming".

"It is your duty to package your offerings to the extent that clients leave your hotel satisfied. Always remember that what makes one rich is not the first business, but the repeat businesses. You must introduce mechanisms that would make your clients' always come back. This is an aspect of your job you must not leave in the hands of your subordinates. You are the chief image maker of your organisation. It cannot be delegated. Marketing is the engine of any business venture. You must go out of your way to learn the psychology of marketing and the strategies you will adopt to put your chain of hotels in the minds

What a Billionaire Told a Poor Man

of many. You are even lucky. During my time, marketing was very difficult. But, with the advent of internet, life has been made much easier. In the days of yore, the world was a global village. But, today, it has been reduced further to a global clan. Get acquainted with all social media platforms. Facebook is the largest assembly of people. Never underrate the impact it is making in the market place. There are others like, Twitter, Instagram, Google, Tencent, Pinterest, YouTube, Viber, WhatsApp and, a host of other social platforms. Maintain an account with all of them and use the social media to drive your hotel business. I am saying all this because shortly you will be alone piloting the affairs of your hotel business".

You must have a pleasing personality

"More so, to market your services to people, you must have a pleasing personality, you must be cultured and with the right mental attitude. On no account should you get angry with your clients. Your personality must radiate confidence and contentment. You must always wear a cheerful mien. It was said that China admonished her citizens never to open a shop if the person cannot laugh. Psychologists have told us that it takes more than 85 muscles to frown your face and less to laugh. Having a pleasing personality entails that you must live consciously and alive in your environment. You must be a motivator and a problem solver. Your members of staff must look up to you. Avoid any kind of behaviour that will bring your reputation into question. Always refer to our talk on

John Learns The Principle Of Marketing

discipline and self-control. Your dressing should not be taking lightly. Style is the man. Dress to suit every occasion. For example, if you are going to address a team of traders in the market, wearing a three piece suit would not feather your nest. Wearing jeans, a T-shirt and a matching face cap would be more ideal. They will connect with you better."

Always learn peoples' names

"Also, people's names are important to them. You must come up with a strategy to call your clients by their first names. People love it. It makes them comfortable. Carnegie insisted that somebody's name is the sweetest thing in any language. As the owner of the hotels, you are the chief marketing officer of the conglomerate. The poor want to be recognized by the rich. Shake hands with your clients. Discuss with them, but, not about your own interests but theirs. Be a good conversationalist. Find out about their interests and generate discussions along those lines. People like to tell stories about themselves. Encourage them for goodness sake, they are your clients. Make them feel important. Be a charming magnet. For your members of staff, be professional in handling them. From the cleaners to the managers, treat them fairly. Listen to them. Don't be harsh. Introduce a programme at the workplace that makes your staffers to have a sense of belonging. Attend their events like; naming ceremonies and weddings. Create a convivial atmosphere in the work place. Discourage backbiting or gossiping. Don't build a hedge around

What a Billionaire Told a Poor Man

yourself. Always keep your doors open. Human begins cannot be controlled or be teleguided, let the system do the work for you. You are not a headmaster. You cannot be everywhere at the same time. Communicate to all and sundry in an unambiguous manner. Discourage highhandedness from your managers. If you must criticize your members of staff, never do it in public. The sons and daughters of men do better under the atmosphere of praise than criticism". The Billionaire continued. "John, hear me this day. Create a family in your work place. You would not be able to grow the business of your dreams if your workforce is discouraged. Do all within your powers to make sure that your system works. Hire professionals to man strategic positions. Don't forget to make sure that your retirement benefits are competitive within the industry. Introduce a Trust Fund for your members of staff. This fund would be dedicated for the payment of school fees of the children of your members of staff. Above all, sow competitiveness in the minds of members of staff. Openly reward any exceptional staff, both in kind and in cash. John we have spoken so much today. It is my belief that you will remember all this when the time comes".

John was more confused than ever before. He has not been able to fathom where all these lengthy discussions are headed. "Does it mean that the Billionaire wants to hire me as one of his managers? Is he retiring? I don't have any staff at the moment and he continues to refer to my members of staff. Anyway, I will wait to see the end of this". Once again

John Learns The Principle Of Marketing

reading his mind, the Billionaire said, "John, never bother your brain. It will not be long before all these will be made in public. Just tarry.

Let's meet by 3:15am.".

"Sorry sir, I did not get that. Do you mean 3:15pm"?

"No John, I mean 3:15am. You as a businessman, you cannot sleep like an employee. At any given time, you have bills to pay. See you then in the study room".

CHAPTER 8

The Billionaire Reveals Self

How the Billionaire made his money

Chief Godfrey Oko is a Billionaire in any currency of the world. He made his money from exporting Nigerian food stuffs to United States of America and Europe. His elder sister, Mama Grace, who married an American, assisted him through school. While in America, he noticed that Nigerians abroad longed for Nigerian delicacies. After finishing his MBA, at Harvard Business School, he returned to Nigeria and started exporting raw food stuffs abroad. It became so lucrative that he had to establish a restaurant where African delicacies would be served in America. Business was good. The number of containers exported increased in leaps and bounds.

Before this time, his ambition has always been to own and run a chain of hotels in America and Europe where local dishes would be served. With time, he built over 15 five-star hotels in Nigeria alone with over 20 in other major towns in Europe. But, the Billionaire was worried. He married an African American. He has

What a Billionaire Told a Poor Man

four children-three sons and a daughter. Unfortunately, none of them was interested in his business. The daughter married an American and the sons are well established in their chosen careers. Besides, the Billionaire being in his late 70's, energy has started deserting him. His strengths are getting dimmer by each passing day. His earnest desire was who he is going to hand over the business to. He never wanted to sell his business as he has no need for the cash. Before now, he had shopped everywhere for a replacement. He has begged his last son who initially showed slight signs of interest to no avail. He resigned to fate, believing strongly that Providence will throw up somebody possibly from his host of employees. When John showed up, he felt that his prayers have been answered. As if by sheer coincidence, John's chief goal matched his. The Billionaire was internally happy. He needed to teach John all he knows about business and many business battles he had fought in the course of his business life. The Billionaire was happy that John though a first class material is also fast leaner. In the past, John had been able to deputize the Billionaire is some critical meetings and he did creditably well. "John is just a genius, but needs to be properly guided and from the way he has carried out my instructions, he will be a success. Besides, this is the time to wire John among my circle of friends, both politicians and businessmen". The Billionaire decided that John needed to do a crash programme at Harvard Business School to enable him have an international clout.

The Billionaire Reveals Self

John goes to Harvard Business School

He sent for him. John, "I need you to prepare some documents to enable you to travel abroad on a-one-month-crash programme on how to run a business at Harvard Business School, United States of America. John's joy knew no bounds. Thanked the Billionaire for the opportunity. "Go and meet my PA and to have everything sorted out. You will be leaving next week". Unknown to John, the PA has already arranged everything prior to this time. He was waiting for the Billionaire to give instructions to enable him fix the travel date.

The Billionaire invites his lawyer

More so, the Billionaire wanted to have some time to work with his lawyers to effect changes on the Will. The Billionaire has hitherto prepared his Will before John emerged on the scene. In the new Will, the Billionaire intends to give 30 percent of estates to charity, 20 percent to his church 40 percent to his family and 10 percent to John and all his books in the library. Also, the Billionaire gave John one of the Four Star hotels in South West Ikoyi, Lagos-Nigeria. The Will, however, stipulated that John within ten years will pay for the hotel and the proceeds used to sponsor young entrepreneurs in Nigeria.

The Billionaire instructed his lawyer that his decision must be carried out to the letter. The Will also made provision of $200,000 dollars to be given to

What a Billionaire Told a Poor Man

John to run his hotel.

The Billionaire made it clear to his lawyer that his energy level has been on the drastic diminishing returns of late. He pleaded with the lawyer to effect the changes immediately to enable him to sign before he joins his ancestors.

The Billionaire signs the Will

Two days later, the lawyer came back to the corrected version of the Will. The Billionaire went through, satisfied and signed the dotted lines.

The next day, the Billionaire called in his bankers, and another lawyer friend of his, to sign as witnesses while the banker took the sealed document to be kept in the bank's vault. The Billionaire was happy that he has put his house in order.

He picked up his phone, called all his four children and the wife. He also called John to ascertain the time of his flight as he has finished the programme in Harvard Business School. He went to his bar, took a shot of hot drink and congratulated himself for job well-done.

Around 8 pm, John arrived from the United States of America.

CHAPTER 9

Billionaire And John Part Ways

By 8am the next day, both met for the first time in the sitting room. Paintings of Jackson Pollok were lavishly used to decorate the wall. They hugged each other. However, John noticed that the Billionaire was looking distant and frail but still with bouts of energy. John, however, narrated all he learnt from Harvard.

"Sir, do you know that all I learnt in faraway America, you have taught me"? The Billionaire smiled and reminded John that he was also a product of the same school.

"The good thing about the school is that the lecturers bring in their own experiences to bear on their lectures. This is because, most of them own businesses. It is not about theories. Most principles are tested in the classroom".

The Billionaire continued, "I am happy that I have taught you well. Even if you don't see me the next morning, I am sure that what you have learnt from me and Harvard will perpetually keep you ahead of competition.

Oh, don't forget that learning is a continuous

What a Billionaire Told a Poor Man

process. You can't learn enough. Good books are good. I don't need to remind you that it is said that many perish for lack of knowledge".

Putting more than you take out

"Lest I forget, there is one more thing that you need to learn before my light finally dims. It is called 'Putting more than you take out'.

Sons and daughters of men are reluctant to make sacrifices. It is an established fact that most artisans do not deliver on time lines. They always fail to deliver as an when due. Employers of labour are consistently looking for employees who lose conscious of time at the work place. Most times, they come to work late and always in a hurry to leave".

The Billionaire continued. "Ability of putting more than you take out is a habit few sons and daughters of men are ready to imbibe. The moment one does more than is paid for and renders services more than is expected; the world stands still for such a person and cannot lack clients.

Many are lazy and prone to reap where they did not sow. They love public holidays without acknowledging the fact that someone would be paid for not coming to work".

"You see, I have stayed here for long and have built companies from scratch. I have hitherto taken unknown firms to IPO level. Listen to me and obey my ordinances. Those with this rare habit always climbs to the pinnacle of their career.

They are not working to impress their bosses. It is

Billionaire And John Part Ways

innate in them. They love the work and never complain.They undertake those tasks that the majority of employees loathe to touch

By forces unknown to man, Providence seems to encourage and compensate them. Such people are never bothered if their immediate boss rewards them or not, but, they continue to trudge on".

"John, though, I have seen the resemblance of their quality in you, but, you need to sharpen the skill to be felt by anybody who comes in contact with you.

In case you become an employer of labour in future, search diligently for those that possess this quality. Groom them and never allow them to go. They are assets.

Before you promote anybody, this must be the chief quality you must consider before elevation.

The Law of Increasing Returns and Law of Compensation will come handy to reward such great characters.

Young man, shop for them, employ them, train them and your organization would be a success".

The Body

"Remember that man lives in three planes- body, mind and soul. You don't need additional lectures on the plane of the body. The only thing I will add here is that you need to be careful with the kind of food you take. Make it a rule that any food you take must contain vegetables. Also, make fruits your friend. Drink water at all times. Go for comprehensive

What a Billionaire Told a Poor Man

medical test at least twice a year. Locate a good physician and cultivate him".

The Mind

"Regarding the mind, my son, read books. Read business books, political economy, history, finance, biographies, autobiographies, financial intelligence, and books on how to run businesses. Attend seminars and workshops. Listen to motivational tapes. Man starts to die when he stops reading. Listen to world news. Make friends with those in government. Study each year's national budget with keen interest. Don't be known with any political party. Romance with politicians, but not intimately, and don't always go to their houses. Allow them to come to you. Entertain them lavishly when they come. They are show people. Choose two leading political parties and secretly sponsor them. Be discreet. Always remember that you are a businessman".

The Soul

"For the soul, always be there for the less privileged. Remember the Good Samaritan. Understand the God of your realization. Be careful of charlatans. Be at peace with both God and man. Don't ever work against the interests of others. John, always go to church and participate in her activities. Endeavour to sponsor church programmes, especially youth related. Create an identity; wearing white clothing would not be a bad idea. Don't be late

Billionaire And John Part Ways

to church and as a rule, always sit in the front seat. Also, remember the widows".

Breathing

Plant trees around your compound. Nurture a garden. There are many ways to breathe. I will allow you to figure this out. Keep your bed near a window.

Science tells us that we need eight hours of sleep daily. No matter how busy you are, John, find time to sleep. Good health is wealth.

Above all, not by choice but a compulsion, you must exercise at least three times weekly"

As he was talking, John noticed that his voice was becoming dimmer. He was barely hearing him. He had to bend towards him.

The Duo sign agreement

"John, my time is up and before I go, we must sign an agreement. John quickly interrupted him. "Boss, you are going nowhere. Your time is never up. Reject it, and I bind it".

The Billionaire smiled, rummaged from the table drawer and brought out a document.

"You see, you must sign this. This is the only payment I would want from you. Recount how you came here and the success I have made of you. Promise me that you will be able to train another person just the way I have trained you. Don't bother how you are going to find the person. The God of your heart will reveal the person to you when the time

What a Billionaire Told a Poor Man

comes. The chain must never be broken. Cross your heart and swear. Let no man or spirit dislocate the chain. I am under an oath to make sure the process continues. Please don't break it.

After training the person, give him $100,000 dollars or its equivalent to start his own business". John was about to interject, but the Billionaire raised his hand to keep him quiet. He continued. "Don't worry where the money will come from. It will be made available when you need it. Also, you must extract the same kind of agreement from the person you are going to train.

You must keep an eye to the funds that I have earmarked to fund entrepreneurship in the country. I have made you the chairman of the Trust Fund. This must be done in memory of me.

Another wish please! Please, make sure that my copy of this agreement must go with me no matter where I may go. I want it to be a reminder that I signed an agreement with you".

Suddenly, the Billionaire started coughing and summoning all the energy in him, he said,

"One more thing, amass every available literature on how to visualize your goals. This is a key to success. Learn to be alone once a day. It is written, 'Be still and know that I am the Lord'.

Once you are alone repeat this affirmation aloud as many times as you can. Let your voice resonate. 'God is my Infinite Supply and money forever circulates freely in my life'

At this point, the cough became extremely persistent and the Billionaire mustering his last

Billionaire And John Part Ways

energy, he said, "John, quickly call my PA. Tell him to come immediately".

Before they came back, the Billionaire has passed on.

John cried and refused to be consoled until dawn.

TO BE CONTINUED
Part two will tell us if John succeeded or not.

REFERENCES

1. Prosperity Bible by Napoleon Hill, Benjamin, Franklin, James Allen, Wallace D. Wattles, Ernest Holmes, Florence Scovel Shinn and Others.
2. The Success Principles by Jack Canfield.
3. How to Prosper in Hard Times by Napoleon Hill, James Allen, Joseph Murphy, George Clason and Money Others.
4. As a man Thinketh by James Allen
5. The Power of your Subconscious Mind by Joseph
6. The Richest Man in Babylon, by George S. Clason
7. The Science of Getting Rich, by Wallace D. Wattles
8. The Holy Bible
9. Merriam Webster Dictionary
10. Brainy Quotes Portal
11. Good Reads Portal

www.ingramcontent.com/pod-product-compliance
Lightning Source LLC
Chambersburg PA
CBHW030806180526
45163CB00003B/1158